THE
RENEGADE COOK

Uncommon strategies for standing out,
stepping up, and making more money
in any kitchen

by
Matt Nelson

foreword by
Tim Kirkland

First Edition, 2015

Published by Terrapin Press
600 17th Street
Suite 2800 South Tower
Denver, CO 80202
USA

terrapin press.

ISBN: 978-0-9969008-0-5

BULK DISCOUNTS / CUSTOM PRINTING

Contact **info@terrapinpress.com** for discounts on the retail price of this title based on quantity.

You can private label a cover for this book with your organization's name and logo or tailor the content to your specific needs and business.
Contact **info@bearenegadecook.com** for details.

Dedicated to all the *Renegades* with whom I've worked over the years and all those who make their living in restaurants, bars, and hotels everywhere.

And to Erin,
Cooper, Sawyer, and Porter,
who inspire me to be better
than I ever could be on my own.

Also dedicated to all the baristas in the world.
I'm sorry I drank all your coffee.

"For far too long the kitchen team has been overlooked and under-served by foodservice consultants and leaders. *The Renegade Cook* resolves this oversight, going beyond temps and ticket times to deliver a valuable, creative, and fun step-by-step guide for what it really takes to be successful in the Heart of the House. Read it and reap!"

- Jim Sullivan
Founder and CEO, Sullivision.com

"Matt Nelson has written the recipe for the perfect cook! *The Renegade Cook* is a concise conversational guide to advancing a career in the Heart of the House. Through simple, engaging direction, Matt breaks down exactly what's needed to turn potential into profits for cooks and managers alike."

- Jason Marx
Kitchen Manager, Illegal Pete's

"This book has a lot of great ideas that felt familiar but were great to see explained in the way they were. I definitely felt motivated and reenergized in my career goals after reading it."

- Joe Reinis
Restaurant Trainer

"As a young cook, I learned these lessons the hard way. If I had read *The Renegade Cook* I could have made my own luck a lot faster. Matt offers sound advice to help cooks understand the restaurant business and get the most out of it."

- Craig Baird
Market President for 70 Applebee's
Franchise Food & Beverage Council Member

FOREWORD

"The definition of insanity is to do the same thing over and over and expect different results."

This quote, often attributed to Albert Einstein, identifies the reason so many people are going 'insane,' or are frustrated, unhappy, or bored at work or stuck in "dead end" jobs. They show up every day for their shift, apply the training they received when hired, do pretty much exactly the same thing they did the day before, and then go home. Repeat.

What these poor souls are missing is that progress, success, and even happiness at work lie in a few simple facts...

- Your basic job training was not designed to make you successful. It was designed to make the restaurant you work in successful.

- Executing on that training will keep you employed... the things that keep you happy, successful, and moving forward are outside of and in addition to that training. And they're entirely up to you.

- Mastery of the skills required for your position will almost never get you better schedules, more money or promotions. Mastery gets you a place on the team. Quality, accuracy and consistency are not unique and spectacular things in the restaurant business. They are oxygen. They're so necessary and fundamental; we couldn't even exist without them.

FOREWORD

- If you want to be different, feel differently about your job and earn different (better) money...you have to act different. In the words of Apple founder, Steve Jobs, you have to *"Think Different."*

If you are holding this book in your hands, it's a good sign that you've decided to start piling onto your basic training additional thoughts, behaviors, and ideas that will help you differentiate yourself at work and achieve better results.

When I wrote *The Renegade Server*, I was looking for ways in which Servers could stand out and differentiate themselves in the eyes of their Guests. As tipped employees, the way to make more money was not to simply deliver the same "steps of service" as every other server (a sure fire way to get *tipped* the same as every other server). It was to find ways to connect with their Guests and to get noticed by adding extra, unexpected behaviors to their routines that would ultimately make them more money.

Like the Server book, *The Renegade Cook* focuses on standing out and differentiating yourself in the eyes of those who affect your success in the kitchen most...your teammates and your managers. And there's no one who knows better how to do that than Matt Nelson.

I first met Matt when we were both working for a national casual dining chain writing training: he for the Back of the House and

FOREWORD

me for the Front. We quickly realized that we shared not only a passion for the business, but a similar approach to training and eerily comparable (if not good) senses of humor.

Since the publication of *The Renegade Server*, I have been asked hundreds of times when I was going to come out with something for the Back of the House. I definitely saw the need for it...trouble is I have very limited experience and expertise with restaurant kitchens. But Matt has plenty, so when he proposed *The Renegade Cook*, I jumped at the chance. It has been a joy working with him and watching how he was able to pour his years of kitchen experience, vast training knowledge, and love for the business and the people who work in it into the Renegade format and philosophy.

This book is long overdue and much needed. I hope you enjoy and benefit from the dozens and dozens of real, easy to use tips and tactics laid out for you in *The Renegade Cook*...written and delivered to you by a seasoned pro who has spent a lot of time in your clogs.

Tim Kirkland

CEO, Renegade Hospitality Group

INTRODUCTION

When I first read Tim Kirkland's *The Renegade Server*, I was impressed. Not just because the tips and techniques he shared somehow struck just the right balance between common sense and new approaches, but because he wrote a book *for servers*. There are so many books and videos out there for managers and executives – more than I can count. Some of them indeed have great information about building sales (and therefore tips), but Tim took his ideas directly to the people who could use them.

That's why I wrote *The Renegade Cook*. There is no group more overlooked and under-supported in the hospitality business than those in the Back of the House. There are lots of reasons that could be true: more attention is given to those who interact with Guests, managers tend to have less kitchen experience (rising up from the ranks of the Front of the House), and culinary jobs are perhaps more process-driven – like following recipes – and there-fore observed or managed less. But cooks are still people, and this is a people business. Cooks are responsible for a gigantic part of the reason Guests eat out – the <u>food</u> – and their development mustn't be ignored anymore.

We no longer live in a world where restaurant employees are "a dime a dozen." Job-seekers are becoming more and more selective about where they work; having opportunities to earn more money and move up the ranks can greatly influence their choices. But there is little training for cooks to develop their skills and behaviors after their initial training – we simply teach them how to cook some recipes and then hope they show up for work every day.

The ideas in this book are meant to change that. There are limitless opportunities within for line cooks, chefs, dishwashers, and prep cooks to make more money, get promoted, feel more fulfilled, and have fun at work. It's the only book of its kind written for kitchen workers, and the ideas inside provide some powerful techniques for accomplishing new and bigger achievements.

This book, however, is not about revealing all the answers. It's about evaluating yourself and how you work, amplifying strengths you already possess, and building a positive reputation at work. *Reading* the book is not going to bring you success – *acting* on what stands out to *you* in the book will.

Many cooks believe that, once they have learned the basics of their station and the recipes and the rules of food safety, they have "arrived."

The truth is, you have just arrived.

INTRODUCTION

Big-time success does not come from *following the rules. Following the rules* is how you **keep** your job, not how you **excel** at it. Following the rules is as basic as turning on kitchen equipment. It's where you take your break or what you wear to work.

True success does not come simply from *following the rules.*
Never has.

Success comes from *mastering* the rules and then
building upon them.

The cook who gets rewarded in your kitchen is not the one who brings food up to the exact correct temperature. It's not the one who uses a measuring cup. It's not the one who puts on gloves at the right time. The cook who gets rewarded isn't the one who simply does what their training tells them to.

Every kitchen has a leader or two. Who is that person in your restaurant? I bet it's the one whose motor is always running. The one who holds teammates accountable. The one who communicates well with the boss. The one who can run a station perfectly and still manage to help someone else.

It's the one who stands out for their character – and that character, combined with the abundance of tips inside this book for moving ahead in your career, is what will make you a *Renegade Cook.*

INTRODUCTION

I'd like to give my thanks a thousand times over to Tim Kirkland. With *The Renegade Server*, he blazed the path of speaking directly to restaurant workers at the front of the action and helping them achieve great success. To me, it shows how much he cares for the "little guy" – and his collaborative style has appealed to countless servers and bartenders, as well as to those who lead them. While this book is its own creation with its own audience, Tim taught me what a Renegade is. Bringing culinary workers into the Renegade family and helping me clarify the message will forever deserve my gratitude. Tim's success speaks for itself, and he offers endless resources on his website, **renegadehospitality.com**.

I also want to thank all of the many dishwashers, prep cooks, line cooks, chefs, and kitchen managers I've met and worked with over the years. Each of you taught me something about the kitchen experience that I wouldn't have seen in the same way, and those lessons have worked their way into these pages.

Matt Nelson

Renegade Author

Cooks: How to Get the Most from This Book!

Every valuable chapter defines certain challenges and truths about working in the modern restaurant environment as well as specific ideas for achieving new successes. To begin realizing these benefits right away, take advantage of the following:

1. Each chapter starts with a preview page that states the specific challenges addressed within. Take a moment to read these overview statements and determine how *they compare with your own experience.*

2. Each preview also lists the specific techniques that explain how to address those challenges. Consider what tricks and tools you already use to accomplish these "how to" steps.

3. Highlight the steps and techniques *that appeal to you.* Apply them one or two at a time for several shifts, giving each your full consideration and attention. Are people reacting differently to you? Keep the ones that begin to feel comfortable and show results and lose those that don't fit.

4. Stay focused on the tips that can help you now. Write out one or two short term goals to work on first. Beware of trying to do everything at once, as it may dilute your execution of any one technique (and your success).

LEARN MORE. EARN MORE.

5. Each chapter contains various "Sidework" side bars designed to make you think about the way you currently work. Think about them and ask yourself what you do well and don't do well – then improve.

6. At the end of each chapter, you'll find a summary. Jot the review points down and look back at them later so you can focus on them during your shifts.

7. There are blank Notes pages in the back. Every time you read something and an idea pops into your head, go write it down in the back. If you don't, you might forget the best idea you ever had!

Share your Renegade successes with us:

Email: **info@bearenegadecook.com**

Twitter: **@BeARenegadeCook**

LEARN MORE. EARN MORE.

Managers, Supervisors, & Trainers

Share the secrets of *The Renegade Cook* with your entire team! Teach everyone on your Back of the House team how to:

- stand out from the rest of the team

- build a reputation of trustworthiness and friendliness – even with the FOH

- learn what a good job looks like – and then perform to those standards

- grow their leadership skills

- be in position for a well-deserved promotion

1. Use the Chapter Previews to initiate discussions during training or one-on-one conversations about the qualities of a Renegade Cook.

2. Encourage positive relationships between BOH team members and between the BOH and FOH. If you run sales contests, pair a cook with each server so they can be involved and help drive competition for the reward. Sponsor fun events that give your team opportunities to interact in a social environment.

LEARN MORE. EARN MORE.

3. Ask team members about nice things others have done for them at work. Talk about how to "pay it forward."

4. Help identify specific ways your Renegade Cooks can help you control costs. Make a plan together for improving those areas - don't forget to set milestones and realistic goals.

5. For more ideas, check out the Extra Bonus section at the back of this book.

Looking for more information on how to create Renegades on your teams? Need more tools to keep the conversation going and develop the future leaders in your kitchens?

We can help embed *The Renegade Cook* into your current training or develop custom training programs for you! Contact us for more information on custom training, consulting, volume discounts, and licensing.

Email: **info@bearenegadecook.com**

Web: **www.bearenegadecook.com**

THE RENEGADE COOK/Table of Contents

Uncommon strategies for standing out, stepping up, and making more money in any kitchen

**"Why join the navy…
when you can be a pirate?"**

Steve Jobs
Apple, Inc.

CHAPTER ONE
TURN UP THE HEAT

Preview

1. Typical cooks are everywhere – and they're going nowhere.

2. Becoming a better cook is the first step of transforming into a *Renegade*.

3. You can have more fun and make more money at work by standing out.

4. Restaurant success comes from putting Guests first, and your success will follow.

5. Your focus on Guests is put to the test during the rush.

6. In this chapter, you'll learn if you're ready to commit to being a better cook and how the characteristics of *Renegade Cooks* can get you there.

Find out what *Renegade Cooks* are made of, then become one.

Are you the best cook at your restaurant?

Let me rephrase that, because it doesn't really matter if you're the best at cooking.

Are you the best employee in your kitchen? Are you someone others like to work with? Do you solve problems? Are you "always there" and ready to help?

Maybe you already act as the leader in your kitchen, make more than anyone else, and get whatever schedule you want. But if not…

…you might be a *typical cook*.

Typical cooks clock in, cook, clean, and clock out. They're everywhere, and they can be pretty hard to tell apart.

Typical cooks:

- have little or no formal culinary training

- learn mostly from peers

- have inconsistent job training

- aren't managed closely

- often have unclear or unenforced standards

- have only developed the culinary skills needed to do their job

- aren't sure how long they'll work in kitchens

And that's *great news.*

Why? Because once you're a *Renegade Cook*, it's going to be so easy to stand out from the crowd.

Why Be a Cook?

I don't remember the moment I first considered myself a cook. It was more like a certain pattern of employment in restaurant kitchens established itself, and from that point on I only looked for line cook jobs.

For a lot of us, it's a matter of convenience. Restaurants are everywhere, and they're almost always hiring. More importantly, they're almost always hiring young people. There are limited opportunities for teenagers to find work, but the restaurant industry hires a *lot* of them: about 1.5 million individuals between the ages of 16 and 19. They make up about 16% of the restaurant workforce.

But you kind of have to be a certain type of person to be a cook. We can be a little rough around the edges. There are some common threads: we often work unusual hours and have flexible schedules, we can handle a physical job, we can follow complex instructions, and we like free food.

One great reason to be a cook is the unlimited job market of the restaurant industry. You'll always be able to find a job. From there, there's at least a reasonable chance you can earn raises or promotions.

Beyond that, you might like being a cook because:

- you love the people you work with - crazy, dramatic, witty, dynamic, fun *restaurant people*

- there's the immediate gratification of cooking: you make the food, and someone enjoys it right away

- you know when your job is finished - there are no more orders

- you like serving others

- you actually love working with food

Food always tastes better when someone else makes it.

My second year of college, I showed up at my advisor's office and told her I was considering dropping out to go to culinary school. I loved my advisor: a quiet but funny woman who taught literature and was writing a novel about her experiences during the Chinese Cultural Revolution. I had a ton of respect for her, and she gave me very detailed (and lengthy) feedback about my attempts at poetry and fiction. She was very disappointed in me at that moment, however.

"Why would you play with food when you can play with words?" she asked me.

Anyone who has cooked for someone else can answer that question. It is art. It is creation. It is service. It can be repetitive, yet each plate is still unique. Even at chain restaurants with recipes that leave no room for interpretation, you're still creating with a medium that is perishable. And there is a sense of accomplishment that comes from making a perfect sub sandwich, just as there is from finishing a beautiful poem.

The point is, if you're going to cook, you must enjoy it at least a little bit. If getting through a crazy rush in a hundred degree kitchen when someone didn't show up for their shift - and just crushing it - doesn't get you fired up even a little, you might want to look around for something else.

What's your favorite part of working in a restaurant?

We cook because it's fun. We cook because it's challenging. We cook because we can – and not everyone can.

Why Be a Better Cook?

Whether being a cook is a long-term plan, or just what you're doing for the moment, you might as well be the best you cook you can be while you're doing it. If you treat the job like it's a waste of time by just showing up and phoning it in, you will fail. On the other hand, if you show up every shift and give it your full focus and attention, you will win. You'll get better schedules, bigger raises, and more promotions.

You'll also have less stress and more fun. No matter how much you enjoy cooking, it's a tough job. It's physical, stressful, and emotional. And, as if the job itself weren't hard enough, you have to work with other people.

Have you worked in other kitchens? Write down a few of the best skills you brought to your current job from other restaurants.

Would you say you like working with other people? Some of the best cooks I've ever met – that is, the ones who cooked the best – just absolutely hated working with other people. But it's a necessary part of the job, so there's constant conflict for them.

Renegade Cooks minimize that conflict. They develop the skills needed to work well with other people. They anticipate and prevent most of the drama, tension, and conflict that can arise between coworkers before it ever starts. And when there is a problem, they resolve it quickly, almost painlessly.

Anyone can develop these skills. Anyone can create a happier work life and earn more raises and promotions. Anyone can be the best cook in the kitchen – a *Renegade Cook*.

The Renegade Cook

A renegade is loosely defined as one who breaks from tradition and commonly held beliefs. A renegade is a rebel, an outlaw.

The *Renegade Cook* is one who masters the basic training that everyone else is using, then steps up his or her commitment, attention to detail, and teamwork in order to stand out, have more fun, and make more money.

Knowing how and being able to do your job correctly is not what makes you successful…it is only the "ante" into the game – the minimum bet required to play.

To become a *Renegade Cook*, you must find ways to "up the ante" of basic restaurant training. You may think that once you have completed your training program and can do everything perfectly in the kitchen you have "arrived." Truth is…you have *only arrived*. It's what you do beyond your standard training that truly delivers success. It's what you do with the rest of this book that will make you a *Renegade*.

What would be the number one thing you would look for when hiring a cook?

Job Description for a Renegade Cook

Do you ever read job descriptions for line cook positions? They're pretty similar – hopefully you can lift 50 pounds and stand on your feet – but they're actually useful, too. They sometimes tell you what equipment you'll be using, what experience you need, and in general, what's important to the people hiring you – the characteristics you need to be a great fit.

These are the general characteristics we're looking for in candidates:

- a desire to become the best cook in the kitchen

- the ability to enjoy working with other people

- a desire to have more fun at work

- an interest in earning raises and promotions faster than anyone else

We put together a job description for a *Renegade Cook*. Candidates should possess the following traits to meet the requirements for our job description:

Passion

If you are going to cook food for other people, you have to have passion for it, for that act of service. It comes from inside, and no one can take responsibility for your passion but you. Furthermore, no one can give it to you. You must create it and foster it yourself.

It doesn't matter if you're cooking something from a dollar menu. Make it with care, and make it with love. Make it the best dollar that customer ever spent.

"Bad food is made without pride, by cooks who have no pride, and no love."

Anthony Bourdain

Standards

Get to know every detail of standards like food safety, recipes, and behavior, and follow them like your life depends on it. Recognize which decisions are *not* yours to make.

Presentation

The final look of everything you make should be carefully crafted, as if you were arranging a bouquet of flowers for a wedding – even if it's just a chicken sandwich. Customers should be delighted at their first impression. Prepare food consistently from shift to shift and according to the recipe.

Communication

Talk with your coworkers. Good kitchens are full of chatter, usually variations of "I need..." and "Got it." *Call* and *response*. I don't trust quiet kitchens, especially cooks who say they "just know" what they need to do. On the other hand, kitchens shouldn't be too loud – anger and panic are distractions. But somewhere right in the middle, a rhythmic blend of ticket status and reminders and ETA's: that's the sweet spot. When called to, always let people know you heard them.

Timing

Sell all food on an order at the same time. Start cooking items at just the right time; too soon, and they can die in the window, too late, and the other food on the order dies.

Handle a Rush

Lead others by being a voice and vision of calm and confidence. During high-volume or stressful times, finishing current orders is more important than starting new ones. Double your communication at these moments, especially about timing. Anticipate product shortages. Respect your team members, especially those in the FOH: the ones actually interacting with customers. The best don't break! They can cook fast and still do it right.

Consistency

Renegade Cooks are predictable. Coworkers know what to expect from them: consistent execution at a high level. And we're not

"Each action in the kitchen requires but a few seconds. It is almost as though the cooks are working on twenty assembly lines simultaneously - each requires a different action. It also requires remarkable coordination among cooks."

Gary Alan Fine, *Kitchens: The Culture of Restaurant Work*

just talking about doing things the same way every time (especially when no one is looking). Renegades are also consistent with their behavior – there's no roller coaster of emotions, no drama. This predictability in how you interact, respond, and behave brings added confidence and calm to your teammates. It is the core building block of trust.

"A chef has a relationship to food, and the cooks who cook it and the servers who serve it, that must be consistent as well. To be consistent in food, as in any relationship, you need rules."

Scott Haas,
Back of the House

Attention to Detail

In the kitchen, there is one thing that can erode excellence in flavor, presentation, and even cleaning – taking shortcuts. When you take a shortcut, you choose not to do something you know you're supposed to do. It can happen when you're busy, when you're lazy, or just when you think you won't get caught.

So catch *yourself*. Don't let yourself take short-cuts. Details matter. The results will show up (either way), and your craft will improve – as will your reputation.

Besides, shortcuts don't actually work.

The things you neglect, sweep aside, or ignore have a way of piling up and becoming real problems that require even *more* time to correct. If you didn't have time to do the job right the first time, when and why do you suppose you'll have time to fix it?

"To do a job well and to do it poorly takes the same amount of time."

San Francisco chef Ruggero Gadaldi

Attack Tickets

Teach yourself to embrace every new order and not hate the ding on a monitor or screech of a printer. We can come up with all kinds of reasons not to start on an order as quickly as possible: too busy, time for a smoke, doing sidework, about to close, someone else's shift meal, etc. But it's the reason you're there, the reason you have a paycheck, so jump on it! Get it done instead of letting it hang around. The best way to get a job done is to start it.

Awareness

Be aware of everything going on in the kitchen. Most importantly, prevent catastrophes by noticing and taking care of small problems *while*

they're still small. Clean up spills immediately, even if they're not yours. Make sure cooks announce themselves if they're walking with a knife or behind someone. Coach someone who doesn't follow food safety practices.

"It's the little details that are vital. Little things make big things happen."

John Wooden

There's more than safety, though. Is someone late for their shift? Did a delivery not show up? Is a vendor looking for someone to sign an invoice? Did an order get rung in? Let someone know. And if you see it, solve it.

Be Proactive

There are two kinds of cooks. One says, "We're out of soup!" The other hands him a hot back up. Be that *second* cook, the one who can anticipate, the one who acts instead of reacts.

You should plan and be in total control of your shift. Prepare for all contingencies, and you will be in the driver's seat. If all you do is show up and "let the shift happen to you" – no plan, no preparation – all you'll be doing is reacting to problems and putting out fires all day. A victim of your shift. That's a great plan – for being frustrated and exhausted!

Lead Others

Visit any bookstore, and you'll find shelf after shelf of books just on leadership. In the kitchen, leadership comes down to some core behaviors:

- do your job well

- coach others instead of calling them out

- be friendly

- don't whine

Leaders in the Back of the House can take the heat.

Don't criticize a new idea unless you have a better idea!

Leadership is not an innate quality with which one is born. Nor is it simply a position or job title (that's authority). Real leadership is activity, and it can be practiced and deployed by anyone on the team.

In fact, research by Harvard professors Marty Linsky and Ronald Heifetz indicates that the majority of leadership activity on a team is deployed by members of the team, not "managers," and it's typically deployed laterally (leading other team members) or vertically (leading upward to management).

Accountability

If you can do everything we just talked about, you'll make fewer mistakes. But when you do, own them. Listen when someone gives you feedback. Listen with the intent to improve the future, not battle the past. Don't go on defense. It doesn't matter what the circumstances were or if someone else always does the same thing you just did. Nod your head, let them know you appreciate the feedback, and then fix it.

Real Success

Now you have the playbook for a *Renegade Cook* – the qualities that will make you a good cook. But the greatest success doesn't come from being the best cook, it comes from Guests being happy. In our business, success is ultimately defined by just one thing: the happiness of the Guest.

If you focus on the Guests, if their happiness is your definition of success, then all the other technical parts of your job will naturally fall into place. You'll become a *Renegade Cook* and reap all the rewards that come with it.

The best time to show off your focus on the Guest is when you see a ton of them – the rush.

The Rush

Cooking well relies upon repetition. Think back to your first week as a cook. You were learning some new techniques, a lot of recipes, and where all the ingredients were stored. With every order, you became a little better. With each dish, you referred to the instructions less and less often. With each trip to the walk-in, you had to hunt around a little less for ingredients. Eventually, you could hold your own, and might have even started working other stations. Why?

Because repetition helps you:

- cook faster

- make fewer mistakes

- look up recipes less often

- find ingredients faster

- clear tickets fast enough to clean and restock

- help other people on the line

And when does all that repetition help the most? When does all that speed, accuracy, consistency, and productivity become crucial? During the rush.

The rush is what you've been preparing for during every other moment in the kitchen. From the size of the deliveries, to the amount of prep, to the station set-up, to stocking plates and containers, it's all been about the rush. You've put in all that work to minimize distractions during this intense time, knowing that even a 30 second delay to run to the cooler, remake an item, or chop a vege-table can throw you off for an hour, and maybe even put you under...dragging your team, the FOH, and the Guest down with you.

We are different cooks during a rush. There are no side conversations, no trips to the bathroom, no smoke breaks...there is just you and your station. And the adrenaline! Why do you think they call it a rush?

How can you not love it? The energy, the focus, and at the end of it, looking up at the clock to find out how fast the time went. When you and the rest of the line kill a rush, there is no better feeling.

On the flip side, there is no worse feeling than when things go wrong. When orders aren't fired. When something is made wrong. When food goes to the wrong customer. When you run out of that one thing that takes longer to prep than anything else. When you are so deep in the weeds that communication either stops or becomes overwhelming, and trust dissolves.

If you've been a part of *that* rush, you would probably do anything to avoid the experience again. The good news is, you can.

"On-the-fly' is a red alert for a restaurant kitchen...not the best way to cook for service, and it seems to me, in most cases, you should be able to avoid having to do this."

Wayne Cohen, *Cooking on the Line*

Build the Church

There are two parts to a busy period: setting up, and the rush itself. Both parts take equal amounts of focus and attention to detail.

When I was a kid, I often heard the saying: "Build the church for Christmas." For a time, it confused me, but I eventually learned that it's a great metaphor for success in a busy restaurant. I grew up Catholic, and what do you think was the one day a year we saw the most people at church? Christmas. While things get a little lonely some summer Sundays, it's always standing room only on Christmas. So, the saying advises us to build the church to accommodate the maximum number of people who will ever show up at one time. Similarly, you should always get ready for the high end of the amount of business you're likely to have that shift. Always be prepared to be busy! If "being busy" is a reason your kitchen routinely crashes, sooner or later your customers will eliminate that problem for you.

Renegade Cooks are never victims of their shifts. They are the *masters* of them. *Renegades Cooks*

are never surprised by their shifts. They *plan* for them. Here's how:

Take a moment at the beginning of each shift to decide what would make it successful.

Getting Ready

1. <u>Know what to expect.</u> Do you usually work this shift? Are sales similar every time? If not, find out from a manager what the sales projection is. Is anything different this time – a large reservation, an event in the area, good weather, an open patio, a shift in Daylight Savings Time? When you know what's coming, you can plan your shift.

2. <u>Identify your team.</u> Find out who else you're working with. What time are they coming in? What time are they scheduled to leave? Have you worked with them before? What are their strengths and weaknesses? Are the right people in the right stations? Is there someone you might need to help during the shift? Are they the kind of people who show up ready to work, or do they usually need time to warm up? You can make adjustments based on the answers to these questions. For example, you might help someone who you know isn't great at preparation get their station set up.

"Professional cooking... demands teamwork and coordination."

Gary Alan Fine, *Kitchens: The Culture of Restaurant Work*

3. <u>Check your station.</u> Prepare your station like you're going to be on television. Start by organizing, cleaning, and sanitizing. Check all your equipment. Stock ingredients and check back-ups. Finally, check plates, to-go packaging, utensils, and anything else you might need during a rush. Ask yourself: if the restaurant were full the whole time, how long could I cook without interruption? Stock and prepare to go as long as possible without needing to leave your station. If you can make it 4 hours, you're prepared for anything.

If you can prepare yourself like that every shift, you'll have a huge head start on any rush. Now all you have to do is cook...

Working the Rush

1. <u>Communicate.</u> While always important, it's *critical* during a rush. Our heads can only process so much, so it's tempting when you're focused on many things to stop talking to your team. But this is when it's even more important. Think about it this way, you can spend 2-3 seconds answering a call or checking on an item at another

station, or you can lose 2-3 minutes when tickets pile up, timing gets thrown off, and mistakes get made.

Take the time to ask questions and answer calls. Prioritize it. If you notice things getting too quiet, encourage communication by calling out more often.

2. Sell Tickets. The quiet before the storm is over. Tickets are getting rung in every 10 seconds. There is a sliver of panic in the back of your mind. Fear starts taking over, tempting you to make bad decisions...like starting every order that comes in ASAP. Here's the problem: let's say you can safely manage 7 tickets at once. That's your max: you are as busy as possible but not making mistakes; you can fire new items, cook anything in the works without hurting quality, and sell the rest. So what happens if you have 15 tickets hanging, and you're firing items on every single one? Either your food is going to look bad, or it's going to be late. Your focus should be on *selling* tickets so you can continually reduce the number of tickets you have while keeping Guests happy by getting their food out as quickly as possible.

Relationship of Number of Orders vs. Working Orders				
# of Tickets Started	1-3	4-8	9-12	13-16
# You Can Execute Perfectly	1-3	3-6	6-8	0

It's far better to sell a smaller number of tickets than to be a little bit done with a lot of them. In cooking, as in life, the more things we are trying to do, the less likely we are to complete any of them with excellence.

You may have a different philosophy at your restaurant, so follow the rules where you are. But if you have a ticket with all the food sold except for something waiting for French fries, finish that ticket before you do anything else.

3. Reduce Mistakes. Nothing can wreck a rush like a mistake – especially a re-cook. It gets you out of rhythm, it frustrates the FOH, and it kills the whole experience for Guests. Not only that, it can get really expensive. During

a rush at a full-service restaurant, mistakes can add up in a hurry. Let's say a busy hour is $1,000 in food sales. If 3 items get forgotten, 2 are made wrong, 1 is burned, and 4 more are comped to make up for slow ticket times (resulting from having to recook the other items), that's 10 items that couldn't be sold. If the restaurant has a check average of $10, that would be a loss of $100.

So what? No big deal, right? They still made $900 that hour!

Not exactly. The average net, bottom-line profit for a restaurant today is about 5%. So, the restaurant profit on a $1,000 sales hour is actually around $50.

That means when we lose, drop, mess up, or give away $100 in food in 1 hour (which includes the cost of the product, the labor it took to make it, rent, and everything else a restaurant pays for to stay in business), we actually lost the profits from 2 busy hours!

Add to that the mistakes from the rest of the night, and it's easy to see why the vast majority of restaurants fail. Busy nights are supposed to make restaurants the most money, but you can see how just a few mistakes can wipe out all the profits.

Not worried about the restaurant's profits? Well, those profits are what's used to pay you, and it's where your future raises come from, so you should be.

When you start treating the restaurant's money like it's your money, it's amazing what can happen. You'll think of yourself as more of an owner than an employee, and that sense of ownership really shows - not just to your coworkers, but to your boss as well. They'll see it best in the heat of the moment - the rush - when you're the one who can stay calm while keeping up.

Renegade Cooks prepare for rushes and execute during the rush, reducing mistakes and saving everyone – both their coworkers and the Guests – a lot of trouble.

Turn Up the Heat

By now, you probably have a good idea whether or not you want to be a *Renegade Cook*. It'll take some hard work, and you might need to step a little outside your comfort zone. But if you're ready to earn more, have more fun, be first in line for the best schedule, and get promoted, you can make it happen.

You'll need to:

1. Do what you were trained to do - and do it well.

2. Take it to the next level and exceed the basic training you received when you were hired.

3. Care about what you're cooking and "show off" your craft.

4. Keep the conversation going with your coworkers to make sure everyone is on the same page.

5. Take the lead by being aware of what's going on around you, anticipating needs, and respecting your teammates – especially when you're coaching them up.

6. Do your job right and hold yourself accountable. Own up to your mistakes so you can improve.

So, what are you going to do? Are you going to just barely meet expectations, act like everyone else, and "simmer?" Or are you ready to turn up the heat? If so, the rest of this book has the uncommon strategies you need to become a *Renegade Cook* and earn all the rewards that come with it.

Summary

- At best, typical cooks only do what they're told.

- Being a cook allows you to work with interesting people, work a non-traditional schedule, be creative, and work with food, all while serving others. It also gives you tons of opportunities to grow a career.

- *Renegade Cooks* develop characteristics that make them stand out from the crowd.

- If at any time you're wondering what decision to make, ask yourself whether or not it will serve the happiness of your Guests.

- Renegades are never victims of their shifts. They are the masters of it and prepare well for even the busiest shifts.

- You can simmer at work like the other cooks, or you can turn up the heat - you'll reap what you sow.

CHAPTER TWO
KILL 'EM WITH KINDNESS

Preview

1. The relationship between the Back of the House and the Front of the House could use some work.

2. Creating positive relationships with the people who directly serve the Guest helps you build a good reputation not only with your team, but with your boss.

3. In this chapter, you'll learn why it's a good thing to be friendly with the Front of the House, as well as some specific ways to build those positive relationships.

Be the cook people want to work with.

There's a war going on.

A war that started long ago but continues to be fought in the boundaries between the kitchen and counter or dining room. The two sides in this war: the Back of the House and the Front of the House. Age-old enemies.

At least that's the story at some restaurants. At others, there's a relationship, trust, a focus on something entirely different than who's messing up an order or who's stealing food from the cooler. The focus is on the Guest.

At these restaurants, they remember that they're in the *service* industry. The *customer* service industry. And when the entire team is focused on the Guest at all times with singular clarity, there's no time to waste on petty arguments. When you're focused on the Guest, you remember why you have a job, you accept that responsibility, and you crush it. As long as you work in the hospitality business, every dollar you'll ever make currently resides with and will only ever come from the pocket of a Guest.

One more thing - if you ever want to be a GM, you'll need experience in the FOH. You'll need sales-building skills, and being a server or bartender is a great way to develop those skills. So think again about disrespecting the FOH team - you might be part of it someday!

Missing Something

Now, do servers, hosts, and cashiers sometimes seem like the enemy? Sure. They're crabby sometimes. They do questionable things sometimes. For example...

At one point in my career I was a line cook at a casual dining pizza joint. A new host who was probably working her first (and perhaps her last) restaurant job had been standing on the other side of the pass for about 5 minutes, staring at me. Pretty annoying. I checked my tickets and asked if she was waiting for a to-go order for "Bob." She was. I told her it was three tickets down and would be up in a couple minutes.

I thought she would head back to the host station to do some work and then come back, but nope - she stayed right there staring at me. So, I decided to have some fun.

"Hey," I said, "if you're hungry, I can cut a piece out of this pizza and then push the other pieces together."

"Really?" she asked, hopeful.

"No," I said, amazed that she believed me. Then I chuckled inside. She actually thought I was serious. I cut the pizza, boxed it, and put it in the window.

Now, about 45 minutes later, I was doing side-work, and the manager came up to me. "What did you *do*?" he asked me, obviously upset. Well, he was upset because "Bob" had just called, furious, asking why he only had 7 pieces of pizza in his box.

Yep - she actually took it up to the host station, ate a piece, pushed the other pieces together, and sold poor Bob the pizza.

"All the cooks left the kitchen late at night after spending hours on their feet, getting yelled at, cooking at great speeds, shouting, and occasionally getting burned. The floor staff? On their feet as well, and night after night keeping their truest emotions under wraps while they took care of hungry people wanting to feel very important."

Scott Haas,
*Back of
the House*

It's hard to keep your faith in humanity after something like that happens. But even after all the bad experiences you've had with your FOH colleagues, the truth is, there are millions more good experiences - and many of them you don't even know about. I guarantee you've either cooked something wrong or been late on a ticket, and a server smoothed things over with the Guests.

Taking Care of the Guest

Taking care of the Guest is the primary, fundamental work in the hospitality business. The very definition of this industry is to be of service. The FOH shoulders the lion's share of this responsibility, as being of direct service to Guests is their number one responsibility. So, to help your restaurant and your team achieve success, to create an environment where you can advance and earn more money, you should either be taking care of a Guest or taking care of someone who is!

Your success is *defined* by the Guest.

It's not how fast you cleared the rail, it's not getting through a rush, it's not getting the best schedule, and it's not even getting a raise.

It's happy people. Happy Guests. And happy Guests are a natural result of happy, cooperative, focused teams.

There's an old saying that great service can save food mistakes, but great food can never overcome bad service. Your success and the success of the restaurant where you work is inextricably linked to Guest satisfaction. Even if your kitchen turns out a flawless, wonderful product, Guests won't return if you don't have an active advocate on the floor.

"It is not the employer who pays the wages. Employers only handle the money. It is the customer who pays the wages."

Henry Ford

And guess what? You can't make Guests happy without a server, cashier, host, or bartender to help you. Without them, you'd actually have to *talk* to the Guests. And I'm just guessing you'd rather not - you're a cook for a reason.

That doesn't mean you don't like people. In fact, I can think of one group of people you just might like quite a bit: restaurant people. We're a little crazier. A little more intense. And we definitely have more fun at work than someone sitting at a desk. Well, FOH people are restaurant people, too. You know you love them. So stop hating them.

If we're not in this together, we're not in it to win it.

I can give you one very important reason why you should: you will be happier. And if it's not a goal of yours to have a good shift, to be happy, to be less stressed, to have fewer remakes, then maybe restaurant work isn't the best fit for you. A job is a job, but there's no reason you shouldn't show up to work just as happy as when you drive home.

So, how can you be happier at work? One way - and don't put the book down - is to go out of your way to make the FOH staff happier. You play a big part in their happiness. You have control over how you treat them. And if they're spending less time with you (trying to get your attention, or asking for a remake, or checking on a ticket, or waiting on their shift meal), they're spending more time with Guests, making them happy. Which makes the restaurant more money. Which they can spend on your raise.

There are two ways to make the FOH staff happier:

1. Get their food right.

2. Be nice to them.

Let's talk about that second point: being nice. Meanness, tension, or disrespect between the BOH and FOH might have a more negative effect on the restaurant than almost anything else you can do. Why? Because it distracts the people serving the Guests. Or worse, it can infect them with a bad attitude or frustration that may then be *transferred* to Guests.

And let's face it, cooks don't always have the best reputation among the FOH. We're known for:

- Ignoring or complaining about refires

- Not helping with recommendations

- Complaining about modifiers and special requests from Guests

- Complaining about or taking longer to make items we don't like to cook, which can actually keep servers from recommending them (and they might be the most profitable items on the menu!)

- Harboring and sharing a belief that servers make more money but work much less

How do you treat your coworkers? What would they say about you?

- Ignoring the fact that when we make mistakes, it's the FOH who pays a financial penalty in smaller tips

- Not giving credit to the FOH for always being on stage in a crowded, critical dining room

- Getting defensive when people question our food quality or presentation

- Snapping at the FOH for even small, completely normal and <u>predictable</u> requests

Not exactly a glowing recommendation.

What if servers lived in a world where they didn't hesitate to ask cooks a question about how a dish is prepared, or order their shift meal, or check on a ticket time? Or even - brace yourself - ask for a plate to be freshened up or remade? What if they felt empowered to describe, recommend, and sell anything on the menu, regardless of how much the BOH likes or dislikes cooking it?

That's a world where the only thing servers and cashiers and hosts and bartenders have to do is take care of Guests, without any distractions from you. Happier Guests spend more money and come back to spend even more. And in case you didn't know by now, it's a lot easier to get a raise at a restaurant that's swimming in cash.

Mickey Mouse

To make that world a reality for the FOH, you're going to Kill 'Em with Kindness. Just like it sounds, that means even when your teammates aren't on their best behavior, you're going to be as helpful and friendly as you can.

One cook who *didn't* do that really stands out from my time as a manager. He was the fastest cook on the line, and he didn't make very many mistakes. But the FOH hated him. He snapped at them, ignored them, and muttered under his breath when they did something he didn't like.

They were reluctant to approach him or even ask him a question, and he made their jobs harder because of it.

So I fired him.

Or tried to. During his termination, he begged for a second chance. He said he'd do anything to keep his job. So, I told him he had to be like Mickey Mouse. Every shift, every minute, from the time he walked in the door until the time he left. Not just okay to get along with, but *like Mickey Mouse* - a cheerful, animated, happy mouse. The ambassador of magic and fun. The most approachable, friendly character in the entire world. The one who goes out of his way to make other people's days better.

To be honest, I didn't think he'd do it. But from that moment, every minute of every shift, he was the nicest person on the shift. He might have had to force it at first, but he actually evolved into someone who was much more enjoyable to be around. And about a year later, he was promoted to manager and transferred to another location in our company and did great.

Attitude is contagious, good or bad. If you can be like that cook and be the nicest cook on the shift, people are going to notice. Success is bound to follow, whether it's a better schedule, more money, or even just more fun at work.

So how do you go from being just another moody cook to being Mickey Mouse? Just like everything else we discuss in this book, it's about making little changes that add up into something big, something that defines you.

The answer is "yes." Now what's the question?

The List

The following is a list of things you can do to be the favorite cook in the kitchen:

1. <u>When a shift meal is rung in, make it right away.</u> Some cooks pretend they need to clear the rails of Guests' tickets first, because suddenly they're just that important.
    If you're really in the middle of a rush, that's understandable, and they probably shouldn't be ordering then anyway. But if you can't handle 2 Guest tickets and a shift meal, you have other problems. Servers will

get hungry. They will order food. It will have 18 modifiers. It's not a surprise. Make it with love and sell it with a smile.

2. <u>Answer calls from the FOH immediately and be friendly.</u> When the expo or a server calls through the window, snap your head toward them, look them in the eye, and answer the call. They are bringing you a request from the Guest, and your job is to serve the Guest or the one who is serving the Guest. Listen to the request and let them know you're on it. A smile wouldn't hurt either.

Always ask yourself: "Is this a decision to make you happier or the Guest happier?"

3. <u>Fix remakes fast and communicate frequently.</u> There's a temptation when a server asks for a remake to ask what happened. It's important information, but it can wait. At that moment, it doesn't matter whose fault it is, it just matters how fast you can get the right food to the Guest. Obviously, if it was made wrong, make sure it gets made right the second time. But anything else can, and should, be discussed later. We need to learn from our mistakes, but we don't need to play the blame game when it distracts us from taking care of the Guest.

4. <u>Time your food and sell your tickets.</u> Nothing is more aggravating to a server than an order that's all ready to go except for one item that takes another 5-10 minutes while the rest of the food gets cold. When you can finish a ticket, finish it, sell it, and move on. It makes a big difference to time your food so it's all ready at the same time.

"A coach is someone who can give correction without causing resentment."

John Wooden

5. <u>Stock and restock</u>. Don't run out of food. Ever. Stock your station at the beginning of your shift and restock *before* you run out. Stock more heavily on items that are being promoted currently, because the only thing worse for Guests than running out of food is running out of food that we told them to buy in a commercial. If you do run out of something, make it available again as soon as possible.

6. <u>Ask about ticket times.</u> The people who can give you the best feedback on your ticket times during service are your teammates in the FOH. Ask them how you're doing. It shows that you can hold yourself responsible and that you not only welcome feedback, but actively seek it out. They'll trust you and know you're there to serve them.

7. <u>Coach, don't criticize.</u> When someone in the FOH makes a mistake, coach them to help keep it from happening again. Don't yell at them. Don't roll your eyes. Don't tell the other cooks how stupid the server is. If all you do is focus on the failure without offering any plan or suggestion for improvement, you are guaranteeing that you'll have to deal with the same problem again (and forever). Instead, let them know the right way to do it, ask if they have any questions, and move on.

8. <u>Place sold tickets under and in front of the food, facing the servers.</u> I've seen a lot of servers pick tickets out of a pizza. Or have to hunt for a ticket when they see their food in the window. Or hunt for the food when their ticket is sold. There is a right way to sell tickets, and it helps servers know exactly when a ticket is sold and what food goes with the ticket. If you've ever had to remake food because a server took the wrong item, you can see how this helps you, too. Not to mention, it gets food out of your window a lot faster. So place tickets in front of the food on the FOH side, under the food it sells, with all items on that ticket grouped together (unless it means putting something cold like a salad under a heat lamp), with the

ticket facing the server so they can see it and read it easily. This is one of the most helpful things you can do, and you can bet it will get noticed. Even if you use a digital system, you can still group items on the same order together. Sell those orders in order from top to bottom - selling out of order causes incomplete tickets that can't be bumped, sold, and run.

9. Introduce yourself to new FOH team members. Start building that trust. Let them know they can ask you a question at any time. Introduce them to the rest of the kitchen team. And while we're at it, don't forget to say "hi" to everyone who comes on shift as soon as possible. It's a basic, friendly thing to do. It will change everything at work.

Write down 3 ways you can take responsibility for improving your relationship with coworkers.

These are some simple steps to being liked by and fostering a friendly, productive, and profitable relationship with the FOH. Some of it may seem a little excessive, but that just means:

• You'll stand out above everyone else.

- People will turn to *you* when they need help.

- You'll get a reputation as the "nice one."

A reputation like that can be very powerful. I promise you it will be worth it just to work with happier people and be happier yourself.

But if you need a little extra incentive, it's the reputation you'll build as a leader, as someone who works well with other people. You'll be the kind of person who moves up, earns raises, gets a better schedule, and earns a break when you make a mistake.

Go get 'em, Mickey.

Summary

- Servers, hosts, bartenders, and cashiers are your partners in the happiness of your Guests – and therefore, the success of the restaurant.

- There are 2 ways to make the FOH staff happy: get their food right and be nice to them.

- Any cook can be civil to their teammates, but *Renegade Cooks* pour positive energy into their relationships.

- Never give the FOH a reason to fear asking you a question or requesting a remake – ultimately, it's the Guest who will suffer.

CHAPTER THREE
THE RULES
OF RAISES

Preview

1. There are more ways to earn a raise than just working somewhere for a long time.

2. A set of just 4 rules is all that stands between you and a higher wage.

3. Once you meet expectations, you can work on exceeding them.

4. In this chapter, you'll learn the Rules of Raises and what action you can take for each of them, including a ton of specific ways you can redirect the money the restaurant spends on other things to your pocket.

Once you know the rules of how and when raises are given, you can beat them.

If you're reading this, there's a good chance you'll get a raise soon. There's almost as good a chance you'll get another after that in less than a year.

Interested?

"Life is a game. Money is how we keep score."

Ted Turner

Good. Because earning raises is up to *you*. Sure, your restaurant may require a minimum amount of time between raises, or perhaps have policies limiting how big of a raise you can get, but you are in control over whether or not you've earned that raise when the time comes.

Stop reading for a minute and think about this question: What are the criteria - or rules - for earning a raise at your job?

There's a pretty good possibility you may not know the answer to that question. And that's not necessarily your fault...yet. If every restaurant manager did a great job of clarifying expectations for performance - and therefore raises - the world would be a better place. But *from this moment on*, if you don't know the rules for earning a raise in your restaurant, it's *your* fault.

Doing Time

The most basic way to get a raise is to work somewhere for a long time. Show up on time, go through the motions, and manage not to make anybody mad. Eventually, after 6 months or a year, just about everyone gets a little more money. But why settle for just a *little* more money? Why wait for someone else to get around to *maybe* giving you a raise? You can take control and get bigger raises more often - you just have to know how to get them.

Just like the myth that servers earn bigger tips by just doing the basics (like moving plates from one room to another and refilling glasses*), it's a myth that you make your money by clocking in on time, cooking, cleaning, and doing your sidework. Like everything else in life, recognition and reward come from doing *more* than what's expected of you.

You have to shine. You have to do everything that's asked of you *and then some*. You have to stand out.

*To find out how to *really* earn bigger tips, check out *The Renegade Server*.

The Rules

You'll start making more money when you know the Rules of Raises. They're not exactly the same everywhere, but there are some basic truths that help you get there faster:

1. You already get paid for what you're supposed to do.

2. You have to *do* more to *earn* more.

3. Your boss is always worried about spending more labor dollars.

4. Building a case for a raise is up to you.

Get Rich Quick

I was hired at a company with a 6 month performance review schedule, and they usually stuck to it. I got hired at $8.00 per hour. After 2 months, I asked for and got a fifty cent raise. After another 3 months, I got another fifty cent raise. And 3 months after that, I asked for a dollar an hour raise. And got it.

That's a 25% increase after only 8 months. I was making $10.00 per hour when I should have only received one raise of fifty cents, which would have put me at $8.50 per hour. With a fulltime 40-hour schedule, that's an extra $60 per week, or $3,120 per year. What could *you* do with an extra three thousand dollars a year?

"You have to learn the rules of the game... then you have to play better than everyone else."

Albert Einstein

How did I get 3 raises in 8 months? By following a basic plan that put me in the best possible position to earn more money.

The Plan

Now that you know the Rules of Raises, you can react to each of them and come up with a plan to earn your next increase.

The Plan below will get you started, but you'll need to fill in the details and discover ways to execute it within the context of your restaurant.

- *Know* what your boss wants you to do.

- *Do* what your boss wants you to do.

- Stand out by exceeding expectations.

- Save the restaurant money.

- *Ask* for a raise.

Each part of the plan is a response to the Rules of Raises:

The Rules	The Plan
You already get paid for what you're supposed to do.	Know what your boss wants you to do. Do what your boss wants you to do
You have to do more to earn more.	Stand out by exceeding expectations.
Your boss is always worried about spending more labor dollars	Save the restaurant money.
Building a case for a raise is up to you.	Ask for a raise.

Step #1: Know What To Do, Then Do It

Before you can stand out, you have to master the basics. Nobody will care when you do something special once in a while if the rest of the time you're falling short. In fact, at reviews, some managers have a habit of judging you on your worst day, not your best. Reviews are designed to measure how you execute (or fail to execute) day-to-day functions, not your one flash of stunning brilliance. You have to know what your boss wants you to do on a regular basis and do it well – consistently.

"The first step in exceeding your customers' expectations is to know those expectations."

Roy H. Williams

An easy way to find out what your boss wants you to do is to ask to see a copy of your job description. You may have seen one in a job posting or at orientation. Chances are, you haven't seen it since. But a job description is your map to success. It clearly defines what you're supposed to be doing. Typically there's more to your job than setting up, cooking, and cleaning. A good job description not only lists the functions of your job, it also includes the kind of attitude and leadership your boss is looking for.

On your next shift, ask your boss for a copy of your job description. But before he or she has a chance to ask why, tell them it's because you want to make sure you're doing everything that's expected of you. Think about the message that will send your boss. How many other people do you think ever have bothered to take the time to ask (or even care) whether they understand and are delivering consistently on expectations? Look at that! You're already standing out just by caring about the basics of your job. Points, my friend. Points.

You get what you focus on.

Next Level Tip: Do a Self-Review

Once you have the job description, grab a pencil and mark next to each line how well you perform that responsibility on a scale from 1 to 5. Be brutally honest; you are the only person who's ever going to see this. Basically, you're giving yourself a performance review. Not coincidentally, reviews are how most managers decide who gets raises and how much they get when the time comes.

How do the scores look? If you're truly honest with yourself – and if you hold yourself to a standard of 100% perfect execution 100% of the time - you're bound to identify a few things you can get better at. Write them down on a piece of paper and read them over <u>before every shift</u>. That way, you'll start each day focused on what you need to improve instead of just showing up and performing the same way every day.

No one who gives his best ever lives to regret it.

Step #2: Stand Out

We talked about the first part of the plan: you already get paid to do what you're supposed to do. You'll need to know what your boss wants you to do, and then do that. Asking for your official job description, scoring yourself on your performance, and then working on improving your performance every shift is a great way to be the best at the basics and meeting the expectations of the job. The next part of the plan is to *exceed* those expectations.

To get paid more, you need to do more. There are a couple different ways to approach this; you can do more actual work than expected, or you can do what you already do better than anyone else.

What does better mean in this case? It depends on where you work and what your job is. But let's start with some basics that almost all cooks do: clean, set up a station, and cook.

Cleaning

Cleaning: it's boring, it's physical, and worst of all, it's repetitive. But it's also going to get you a raise. Why? It's one of the most visible ways you can stand out. If you clean better than other people, it's going to get noticed. Let's say part of your sidework is sweeping the floor. You could just sweep what's easy to see - the floor that the lights shine on. You'll get most of the trash and food, and the floor will look clean. If you want to stand out though, you need to sweep under all the tables and equipment. Then the floor doesn't just look clean, it *is* clean. You might be able to get away with not doing it most of the time, but once in a while you'll get called on it. And each of those little memories of you not doing your job the right way pile up like French fries under a cooler. Those memories get hauled out at review time.

So clean your station like it's a million dollar yacht. In fact, if pretending it's a yacht helps you clean better, go for it. Play mind tricks on yourself. Do what you need to do to stand out. Make it shine, make it sparkle, make it look like new.

I remember a cook who used to be pretty intense about cleaning (See? I remember him for his cleaning. He stood out!). He always did a number on the broiler, making sure it was scraped, brushed, and seasoned every night. Not only that, he cleaned the fryers like nobody else. He didn't just wipe the top and front, he pulled it out and scrubbed the sides, then *opened the door* and scrubbed all the grease from the inside. Every time. As his Kitchen Manager, when I checked out his sidework on those nights, I'd always say, "Damn it Aaron! You bought a new fryer? We can't afford that!" It was cheesy, but his face lit up every time I said it. More importantly, he made an impression on me because he took pride in his work.

Station Set-Up

Whether you set up a station from scratch or just restock at the beginning of your shift, you can stand out. In this case, it's all about quality and how thorough you are.

Being thorough is actually pretty simple. It means making sure every ingredient you need is prepared and ready to go at your station on time. That might mean when service is beginning, or earlier if you have line checks. Whatever the case, you should be able to prepare every order that comes in without having to leave the line. At least not until well into your shift, when something needs to be restocked. That goes for utensils, too. Cooking is hard enough without having to get out of rhythm because you didn't stock tomatoes or a pair of tongs.

What's one thing you always have to go looking for in your station? Write it down, then make sure your last shift was the last time that will ever happen.

Quality is the second part of a well set-up station. Too many times I've walked the line to see brown lettuce or cheese that's drying out. The ingredients don't need to just be there, they need to be at the highest quality. Customers coming in today are paying the same price as the customers who did yesterday, so they should get food that's just as fresh. When you set up, don't hesitate to replace poor quality food with something better. Nothing looks better at open than a line with every pan full and every ingredient at peak freshness.

If you're a prep cook, the same rules apply for station set-up. As you start your shift, your focus is on knowing what you're going to prep, getting the recipes, grabbing whatever equipment and utensils you need, and, most importantly, giving yourself space to work. Nothing adds more time to prep than not having enough space or not cleaning as you go. For prep cooks, the set-up process cycles every time you start a new recipe. That means your space should be reset with plenty of room and a clean, sanitized station.

You can "get by" without setting up your station with this kind of attention to detail, but doing it the right way consistently will get noticed.

Cooking

Finally, you can stand out when you cook. It comes down to fundamentals and presentation. Cutting corners is the status quo, so even doing the basics here can help you rise above your peers. The goal here is to not have to be *managed*.

Take a moment to think about the times when you're managed right now. Some examples might be:

- arriving late

- not cleaning to standards

- not following recipes

- taking too long to make something

- forgetting a modifier

- doing something wrong after being shown the right way

- poor presentation

These are all fundamentals, especially following recipes. Chances are you've made something different from the way you were supposed to at least once. Sometimes you weren't trained right, but that excuse only works once. The rest of the time, it's just cutting corners.

For us, it may be "just another meal," bur for our guests it is *always* an occasion.

Don't cut corners! That's not how you want to stand out. Follow the recipe, and do it every time.

If sticking to fundamentals is a way to stand out by not being noticed, presentation is the exact opposite. Food presentation is such an important part of the Guest experience; that moment when the food is set in front of them is the moment they decide whether or not they're going to enjoy it.

Presentation has everything to do with that moment. It's the first impression, and Guests can tell if something was put together with care or not. That's the first layer of presentation, the overall appearance of the food: whether it looks sloppy or crafted, old or fresh, like it died in the window or flew from the kitchen to the Guest.

But there's more to presentation than the first impression. Let's use a simple burger as an example. You can tell how much a cook cares about presentation just by flipping over the top bun. Most burger buns are toasted, so a burned bun is a pretty easy way to judge the cook's commitment to quality. It's as if the cook is saying, "I'm not good enough to toast bread, and I don't care about you enough to try again and serve you something better." It's the perfect test, because most burger buns are either served toasted side down or covered up by lettuce, so servers can't tell if they were done right. You can get away with it.

Cooks who "try to get away with it" don't get extra raises.

So if you can pay attention to your presentation, you can stand out. It's about details, and although your menu might not have a burger on it, you can stick to some universal truths about presentation.

Good presentation means:

- Hot food is hot and cold food is cold.

- The Guest's first impression of the food is that it's crafted, not sloppy.

- The ingredients look fresh.

- Plate rims are clean.

- Food is the right color.

- Dishes with height (like salads) are built tall.

- Ingredients are spread evenly (think pizza toppings or sandwich ingredients).

Write down all the costs you think restaurants might have and rank the 3 you think are the most expensive.

Step #3: Save the Restaurant Money

The next part of the plan is to get around one of the biggest obstacles you face: the number of dollars available for your raise. Every Chef and Manager in every restaurant is *constantly* thinking about costs.

The two biggest costs for restaurants are labor and food. Put together, they often account for over half of the money the restaurant brings in, and that's without paying for rent, utilities, beverages, insurance, and 100 other costs that add up to about 90-95 cents for every dollar the restaurant brings in. Controlling labor and food cost is one of the most important things managers do, because they're not fixed (like rent) - they go up or down depending on how well they're *managed*.

There's a clue for you: they need help managing those costs. Often, it's up to the people on salary to control costs by doing things like writing focused schedules, cutting staff, and ordering only what the restaurant needs. If you look back at *your* job description, I bet it doesn't say anything about hitting budget for labor costs.

But that's how you're going to stand out. You're going to help them control costs - with a goal of reducing them. It might be your most powerful ammunition when it's time to ask for a raise. I mean, who can argue with you requesting more money when you helped save the same amount or more?

The best part is, nobody else on your team will be doing it. It's just one more way for you to stand out from the rest of the pack and build your case for a raise when the time is right. And it's really not that hard.

Sure, your teammates in the FOH could generate an extra $1 in sales pretty easily, but remember: all those costs we've discussed get taken out of it. On the other hand, when you help the restaurant save a dollar, it's always worth a dollar!

Finance 101

When we first talked about the Plan, we said you had to meet expectations first. And to do that, you need to ask what those expectations are. It's the same idea here: to help manage costs, you need to find out what they are and what needs to be improved.

Grab your manager for a one-on-one chat at the beginning or end of a shift. It should only take about 5 minutes. Let them know you want to talk about what you can do to help control costs. (Once again, simply asking about them is going to help you stand out as someone who cares about their responsibilities and the restaurant's success.)

As with any meeting, you want to be prepared. In fact, you need to prepare before you even bring it up, in case they're ready to talk to you right away. These are the questions you're going to need to ask to get smart about the restaurant's finances:

1. What's the budget for labor cost and food cost?* (hint: ask if it's the budget just for hourly cooks or the whole team, including managers)

2. Are we hitting budget for labor and food cost?

3. What are some of the biggest impacts to food and labor costs right now?

4. What are some specific things we can do to improve costs?

Write down a list of costs you can help control and review them before every shift.

That last one is the most important, because you're going to write down what they say and add it to your list of things to look at before every shift. It's going to give you clear, specific ways to help reduce costs, and many of them are things you directly have control over.

Cutting Food Cost

One of your manager's answers could be, "We throw away too many tomatoes." If cutting toma-toes for service is one of your jobs, you have direct control over how many tomatoes are wasted. And even this one thing could have a huge impact on costs.

Let's say your manager is right, and you're throwing away too many tomatoes – we'll say 20% of the tomatoes prepped are being thrown away. Now let's say your restaurant buys $200 of tomatoes per week. If 20% of them are being thrown away, that means you're spending $40 per week on tomatoes being thrown in the trash. Do you know how much a $1.00 per hour raise costs for 1 full time employee each week? Yep – it's $40.

So how do you cut down on those wasted tomatoes? There are lots of possibilities, and the answer is usually a combination of a few of them. Some examples are:

- Prepping: slicing tomatoes too thick (getting fewer slices per tomato) or cutting the discarded ends too big

- Rotation: new tomatoes are being used before older ones

- Storage: tomatoes aren't being held at a temperature that slows spoilage

- Prep pars: more tomatoes are being prepped than you can use before they go bad

- Portioning: More tomatoes are being served than the recipe calls for

If you committed to cutting that waste down to as close to zero as possible, you'd be finding the money for a big raise with just one item. You can see how quickly this might add up. If your manager gave you a list of the top 5 most wasted ingredients in the restaurant, you could focus on reducing waste for all five of them, which could result in pretty significant savings for the restaurant.

Remember to get credit for the cost savings. To do that, you'll need to:

1. Ask what products contribute the most to food cost.

2. Commit to your manager that you'll do whatever you can to help reduce waste for those products.

"Some people want it to happen, some wish it would happen, others make it happen."

Michael Jordan

3. Focus every shift on cutting those costs.

4. Follow up a month or two later to see if waste for those products has improved.

Another big way to cut food cost is to reduce *your* mistakes. It doesn't matter if you're on the line or if you mostly prep – mistakes happen, and they result in food getting thrown away instead of getting paid for by Guests.

When food is made for Guests but can't be served or is returned, it's often comped – complimentary – which means it's either never rung in, or it's taken off their bill. The price they would have paid never gets collected, which means the restaurant not only loses the profit, it loses the full cost of the food (as well as all the other costs that go into running a restaurant).

Not all mistakes can be eliminated, but you can score yourself on your mistakes. When are you making mistakes that cost the restaurant money? What's causing them? The answers might be any of the following:

• Not reading the ticket/screen carefully

- Not communicating with other cooks

- Under or over-cooking

- Poor quality ingredients

- Forgetting part of an order

- Serving hot food cold

Isolate the causes of your mistakes and then focus on eliminating them. If you can decrease the amount of free food being served, food cost will be lower, and there will be more money for your next raise.

One last way to bring food cost down is to follow recipes exactly. Most restaurants carefully price their menu so they will make the right amount of profit based on the amounts of ingredients in each item.

Let's look at a pepperoni pizza as an example. The restaurant will calculate the individual cost of each ingredient in the pizza: dough, sauce, cheese, and pepperoni, based on what they pay for each ingredient. If the cost of those 4 ingredients were $2.50 per pizza, they would have

▷
Write down 3 orders you made that were either comped or remade. What happened? What could you have done differently?

to sell it for $10 to reach a 25% food cost for that pizza.

But if you put just 10 extra pepperoni or a couple extra ounces of cheese on each pizza you make, you might be giving away hundreds of dollars of free food to Guests. Just that little bit extra could be $0.50 per pizza, raising the food cost to 30%. If the restaurant sells $10,000 worth of pizzas per week, they're now spending $3,000 instead of $2,500 to make them - losing $500 per week. At a %5 profit margin, that means *zero profits* were made for the entire week!

By following each recipe exactly and only putting on the right amount of each ingredient, you'll help the restaurant spend only the money they planned on spending for everything on the menu.

So, with even a little success in curbing food cost, you'll be well on your way to freeing up some money for your next raise. And the good news is, reducing what's spent on food represents only 50% of what you can do to help control costs in your restaurant.

Cutting Labor Cost

Like food cost, labor takes up a huge chunk of restaurant revenue. In fact, in most restaurants, it's the *largest* controllable cost! You might only be thinking about your hourly wage as the cost to the restaurant of employing you, but there's a lot more to it. They also pay half of your federal income tax, social security, and Medicare. On top of that, they pay for unemployment insurance, worker's compensation insurance (in case of injury), and possibly discounted food, uniforms, and health insurance. All of these pay-related expenses add up to a lot more than your wage.

We're not trying to inspire any sympathy here – but you have to know what restaurants are up against when it comes to how they spend their money. It's why saving the restaurant money can be such a great strategy for making your case to get bigger and more frequent raises.

Can you do anything about the taxes, insurance, and other pay-related costs? No. But you *can* help cut down on the dollars spent on wages, which is what restaurant managers track most closely. In fact, most managers will look at labor costs *daily* (or even hourly) as a percentage of wages divided into sales. The more frequently that number is over budget, the more those managers will be thinking about cutting labor costs.

The primary tools available to management to reign in over-budget labor costs are cutting wages and cutting hours – which means you either need to get the same amount of work done in less time or for less money. Both are very, very bad news for you. All that ongoing stress of constantly worrying about labor costs can wreck everything for you when it's time to talk raises.

You Can't Pick Your Coworkers, but You Can Send Them Home

Every restaurant has a schedule, and that schedule marks out how many hours need to be worked (and paid for) that week. It's based on what they think sales will be like for the week. If sales are higher than expected, usually the actual hours worked go up. And when sales are lower, the hours worked should go down – but they don't always, at least not enough to make up for the drop in sales.

On slow shifts, your manager might try to hurry some of the staff out the door before the scheduled end of their shifts. But managers get busy and distracted, and they don't always get to "cut" people when they should.

That's where you come in. You're going to make it easy to send those people home. You're going to help keep them focused on getting sidework done and whatever else they need to do before they leave. You can even jump in and help them finish up prep, set-up, or cleaning so they can clock out sooner. Why? Because the total hours worked will decrease, helping that labor percentage meet the budget.

What are 5 things you can do to help others finish their job sooner?

You don't just have to do it on slow shifts, however. Even when it's busy, you can help get people out faster by helping them do what they need to do. They'll probably even appreciate the help without realizing it's all part of your covert plan to make more money. Because at the end of a shift, even those cooks who watch every penny on their paychecks don't want to scrub pans and push a broom around. They have plans. They're tired. They want to leave. And *you're* going to accommodate them.

It all comes down to another truth about working in restaurants: someone *always* wants to go home. And if you help get them out sooner, you're not only saving the restaurant money, you're staying on the clock.

Friends Don't Let Friends Get Overtime

Overtime is a killer. It costs the restaurant 150% of what they would have been paying for a single hour of labor. And someone who works that many hours deserves to get paid extra. But it's not helping your cause any.

People who get overtime tend to talk about it. So when you find out a coworker is going to hit over-time, do what you can to help them so they can be sent home. Even if you or another cook ends up working those hours, you won't be doing it at the higher overtime rate, so it won't cost the restaurant extra money.

Asking your manager how you can help is the best way to not only stand out but know exactly what you can do to help. But whether you get credit or not for the times you help save the restaurant money, you're still helping to make room for your next raise. The little things add up, so do your part and you'll clear another obstacle to earning your next raise out of the way.

Step #4: Ask for a Raise

By now you've probably realized that simply waiting for raises doesn't give you the best shot at making more money. The last part of the Plan puts that into the simplest terms: don't just wait for a raise...*ask* for it.

"The man who waits for a roast duck to fly into his mouth must wait for a very long time."

Proverb

By doing everything you've read so far in this chapter - knowing what you're supposed to do, doing what you're supposed to do, standing out, and saving the restaurant money – you'll put yourself in the best possible position to get a "yes" when you ask for a raise.

Remember, it's not about that one shining moment, it's about consistently doing your job and being the person who most deserves a raise. On top of that, you have to ask the right way, which pretty much looks like this:

- Do good work.

- Alert your boss you want a raise.

- Keep doing good work.

"If you work just for money, you'll never make it...But if you love what you're doing, and you always put the customer first, success will be yours."

Ray Kroc

You might not get a raise the first time you ask. That's okay, because if you're doing good work, the money will come. But there's another reason that asking for a raise and not getting it still helps you take control over the situation: the more you ask, the more likely you are to get what you want.

At some point during every weekend, my 3-year-old son asks me for a sucker. Usually it's at breakfast time, so the answer is typically "no." But if he asks me again a couple hours later, it's a lot harder to turn him down. And if I do, he ends up asking again. And I usually break.

It's a lot harder to say "no" to someone 3 times than it is once. That's why a "no" when you ask for a raise isn't a big deal. As long as you do it in a respectful, professional way, and you're sticking to the rest of the Plan, it makes the chance of getting a raise next time much more likely.

If You're Invisible, Make Some Noise

One of the most important parts of the Plan is to *do good work*. I have to tell you a secret: there's a really good chance your manager won't notice. What do managers talk to their staff about the most – what they do right or what they do wrong? You guessed it – what the staff is doing wrong. The people who are *under*performing tend to get the most attention.

That's why you have to make some noise and *ask* for a raise. When you're doing a great job, you'll likely get less attention from your boss. Even if you stand out sometimes, the question of whether you're getting paid what you're worth isn't likely to pop into your manager's head very often. So, you have to get in their face - again, in a nice way. Think of it like you're starting a conversation rather than asking a yes or no question.

Here's a few things to keep in mind for that conversation about your future finances:

- Timing: When you're ready to talk, make sure the other person is, too. Is it a busy time of day? Do they have something urgent to do? Also consider if you have a performance review coming up. If you're within a few weeks of a review, you should probably wait to talk about money.

- Prepare: If you've really had an impact on controlling costs or found other ways to help the restaurant be more successful, be prepared to discuss it. A thoughtful presentation that sums up the excellent work you've been doing can help push your case.

- Respect: Be a professional. Remember, the raise is a result of your behavior and effort. It's a natural outcome of your performance. Don't mess it up with a lack of professionalism. Be patient, be respectful, and be a good listener. If you don't get the raise, you'll want to listen to the reason why so you can work on it.

Earning a raise is a tricky business. Businesses tend to protect their profits, not spend them. But by doing your job well, saving the restaurant money, and *asking* for a raise, you'll triple your increases.

Summary

- There are ways around any roadblock to earning your next raise.

- Knowing the Rules of Raises is the first step on the path of earning more money, and it starts with realizing you already get paid for what you're supposed to do.

- You have to do more to earn more, and you can't do that unless you know exactly what the expectations for your performance are.

- When your performance stands out from everyone else, the limited money available for raises is more likely to go to you.

- Understanding how the restaurant spends money on food and labor enables you to help control those costs.

- Once you've proved you deserve a raise, ask for one – you greatly increase the chance of getting a raise when you don't simply wait around for it.

CHAPTER FOUR
BE THE NEXT IN LINE

Preview

1. *Renegade Cooks* are the best candidates for promotions.

2. The best way to separate yourself from others is to build trust with the people you work for.

3. The way you act and work with others carries a lot more weight than how you perform tasks.

4. Management and leadership are two very different types of skills, and a balance between the two shows you're ready to supervise others.

5. In this chapter, you'll learn how to lead others – even your peers – and then use those leadership skills to become the obvious "next great thing."

Renegade Cooks don't stay cooks forever. Become the obvious choice, then strike at the right moment.

Who are you when the restaurant is slow?

Do you slow down, too? Do you take more time to sell orders when it's slow than when it's busy? Do you look for things to keep you busy, or do you just look out for your boss?

Some of the best advice given to new General Managers is this: "It's not how the restaurant runs when you're there, it's how it runs when you're not."

And *you're* the one running it. The way you perform when no one is looking and the restaurant is nearly empty partly determines how successful the restaurant is, and ultimately how successful you are.

The reason we're leading off with this question is because it goes a long way to figuring out how ready you are for a promotion. Cooks who still kick butt when it's slow have integrity - they don't change their behavior when nobody's looking. They don't take their foot off the gas when it's slow. They don't treat people differently from shift to shift. They're consistent, predictable, and trustworthy.

It's that last word that will separate you from the rest of the pack. To be promoted, whether it's to lead line cook, manager, or sous chef, you have to be trusted. The people you work for need to know they can count on you to:

- show up for every shift

- be on time

- stay as late as you're needed – even if it's past your scheduled time

- pick up shifts when no one else will

- treat people professionally

- be friendly to everyone you see at work: other cooks, FOH team members, managers, vendors, and Guests

- protect the product and money

- be safe

- support the company and its decisions

- be invested in the restaurant's success, each shift you work, for however long you work there

No one will give you the keys to the car if they think you won't take care of it. In this case, past behavior is the best prediction of future behavior: trust is something you have to build. You can't talk your way into it.

A Great Secret Mysterious Truth

I remember a cook who wanted to be the next Assistant Kitchen Manager in my restaurant. He was the lead line cook, he was totally reliable, he didn't cut corners, he could place and put away orders, and he worked more hours than anyone else.

And he *never* got promoted.

Every week or two, he would approach me about moving up. He would talk about how well he cooked, how helpful he was with administrative tasks, and how he knew all our standards. He particularly focused on the fact that when I was away, he would write the schedule and place food orders. Those are important tasks, usually reserved for managers, at least at our restaurant.

"If there is any one secret of success, it lies in the ability to get the other person's point of view and see things from that person's angle as well as from your own."

John D. Rockefeller

So, he demanded to know, if he was the only person I trusted to place food orders, why didn't I promote him?

"'There are also emotional and psychological components,' said Tony, 'I mean, just because someone can cook well and then move up, it doesn't necessarily mean they can lead.'"

Scott Haas,
Back of the House

That's easy: managing *food* is a lot different from managing *people*. That's the Great Secret Mysterious Truth: managing is all about people.

Sure, I could trust him to count how many bottles of ketchup we had, subtract that from the par, and then order the difference. But I definitely couldn't trust him to:

- lead others to a common goal

- treat everyone fairly

- make our culture thrive

- include others in his decisions

- prevent problems from happening

- solve the problems that do occur

- have a sense of awareness that exceeds everyone else's

- prioritize based on the needs of our Guests, then others, then himself

The fact that he didn't even know those characteristics are part of the job says a lot. If you want to help place orders, I'll give you a well-deserved "thank you," and maybe a *little* raise. If you want a promotion, you better know what it takes to earn my trust, and more importantly, what it takes for me to trust you with managing *people*.

"Constantly search out small improvements, not just big ones. Every day get a little bit better."

Jim Sullivan, *Multi Unit Leadership*

Find Out

If you've never worked a job before, chances are you don't know everything it takes to do that job well. That's the situation with a promotion: it's a job that you know a little about but haven't actually done yourself. So if you don't know what it takes to do the job well, what do you think you should do?

That's right: ask!

How do you know you even want that job unless you know more about it? And how are your managers going to promote you if you don't show them that you could be successful at it?

If you have your eyes set on a job – on the next step up from where you are today – you can get it. And because you're becoming a Renegade Cook, you can get it faster than anyone else. You just need a plan.

Perhaps you're noticing a pattern here. Achieving professional success doesn't happen without a plan. *Renegade Cooks* devise plans for improvement, execution, and success. *Average* cooks show up and let the shift, the restaurant, and the work happen to them. Average cooks hope the good things occur and the bad things don't. Renegades *make* it so.

Are there other kitchen positions you can cross-train into? The more positions you can work, the more valuable you are to your leaders.

The first step of your promotion plan is: find out what your job would be like if you got a promotion. There are a couple of ways to do this: you can ask a manager, and you can do some research.

Asking a manager is easy; you just request some time with them one-on-one, find out what position would be the next one for you to advance into, and ask what it takes to be successful at that job. Here are a few questions you might consider asking:

- What makes this position different from my current job?

- Is supervising people part of the job?

- What training is required?

- What other prerequisites are there before someone can be promoted into this position? (like education, certifications, etc.)

- What characteristics would you look for to consider promoting someone into this position?

- How would you describe success for someone in this position?

The other way to find out more about your next job is to do some research. Hop online and see what you can find out. You can look at job descriptions at sites like Glassdoor and Indeed or the career pages of other companies. They'll give you some idea of the characteristics those companies are looking for in their managers.

The Ladder

One piece of advice that has stuck with me over the years is that you have to do your current job well before you can move on to the next one. If you've followed the Rules of Raises, you should have that part wrapped up. The technical skills needed to do your job, also called hard skills, are really important - they're what you get paid for. But to climb the ladder, you'll also have to develop soft skills - the ones used to manage people.

"Management is efficiency in climbing the ladder of success; leadership determines whether the ladder is leaning against the right wall."

Stephen Covey

Actually, you'll be taught how to *manage* people after you're promoted. Management tasks like solving immediate problems and checking people out at the end of their shift are important skills, and they'll be part of your training. But *leading* people is another thing entirely, and there's only so much you can be taught. Becoming a good leader is really up to you and the decisions you make.

Management vs. Leadership

So what's the difference between managing people and leading people? There are easily a hundred different answers to that question. One simple answer is that managers tell people the right thing to do, and leaders influence people to do the right thing.

"Management is doing things right; leadership is doing the right things."

Peter Drucker

Another way to think about it is this: management is a skill; leadership is a behavior.

Have you ever worked somewhere and found out a coworker had been promoted to manager? What happened after their promotion, once they were charged with supervising their former peers? It's a challenging situation – the team may resent having to answer to someone with whom they used to be on equal footing, especially if they think the promotion was undeserved. The new manager might misunderstand their new role and spend too much time barking orders, creating even more tension and distance. It can take a long time to repair the damage.

And that's where leadership comes in. It doesn't replace management, it complements it. Too much of one and not enough of the other is bad, and the most common situation with newer managers is lots of management and not enough leadership.

A common distinction between the two is that management is often focused on the "Now," and leadership is often focused on the "Future."

Now (Management)	Future (Leadership)
Solving immediate problems, such as: • going to the store to buy tomatoes • answering a phone call about donations • talking to an unhappy Guest	Creating a success-ful future, such as: • developing people • building account-ability through a coaching conversation • making a culture of professionalism thrive

Again, you can't just be a leader and not a manager – someone has to talk to that unhappy Guest – but management gets a lot harder without leadership skills.

The New Boss

One of the biggest challenges of getting promoted is becoming the "boss." Whether the staff knew you before or not, you're going to face some challenges in leading them. Even if you were promoted internally at the restaurant you've been working in, you're going to be the "new guy" all over again in your new position. And nobody wants to take orders from the new guy.

I remember moving into a manager role and transferring into a new restaurant where I didn't know a soul. During my tour on the first day, I was shown the walk-in cooler, and it was a mess. Nothing was labeled, containers weren't stacked neatly, and the same items were stored in multiple locations. I wanted to get in there so bad and just tear it up.

But I couldn't. Why? Because there were 20 cooks working there, and if I walked in on Day One and rearranged the cooler, they would have revolted. Can you imagine going in there to look for something, not finding it, and then hearing that the new boss moved everything around on his first day? It would take months to repair that damage. You have to build a relationship first. You have to earn and build trust. Leadership means you have to earn "followship" before you give orders.

When dealing with people, remember that you are dealing with creatures of emotion, not logic.

I eventually got to that cooler and made it look the way I wanted; but first, I communicated a vision for keeping the kitchen organized, and then I invited a couple of the lead cooks to help me and share their ideas. Not only did they feel included, they got others to buy in to the changes. Way more effective than just telling everyone that the cooler had to be organized a new way, don't you think?

Lead Before You're a Leader

So, how can you show that you're going to be a great leader before you get the chance to lead anyone? By demonstrating the characteristics of leadership, which *anyone* can do. You don't need a title to lead people.

There are all kinds of words that might come to mind when you think of a leader. In fact, it's not a bad idea to write them down and think about where you stand on each of them. After all, every leader is different with different qualities. But there are a few that really stand out to me when I think of great leaders in the kitchen: awareness, energy, integrity, and confidence.

Awareness

Everyone has *some* awareness of what's going on around them. Leaders are aware of *everything* going on around them, what happened yesterday, and what's going to happen tomorrow. They don't just hear the ticket printer beep when they're on the line, they hear it when they're putting an order away in the cooler and then think about who's on the line to make it. They are constantly observing what's going on around them, thinking about where people need to be and who needs help.

"If you want your life to be more rewarding, you have to change the way you think."

Oprah Winfrey

More importantly, they focus more on *preventing* problems than solving them. Having a great sense of awareness helps them anticipate needs.

I was reminded of this the other day while at my favorite burrito place. As the last spoonful of cilantro rice was scooped out of the pan, a prep cook was standing there with a full backup. She hadn't been told to bring it up, she had just remained aware of how busy the restaurant was and anticipated when the backup would be needed.

Managers are paid to anticipate, not react. *Anyone* can react to a problem. Have you ever worked with a manager who just seemed to run better shifts? Where nothing really seemed to go wrong whenever they were there? That's because managers like that anticipate potential issues and deal with them before they become problems for either the team or the Guests.

Energy

Attitudes are contagious. You've heard that before, right? I used to hear it at work all the time. Why? Because during one out of every three shifts or so, someone clocks in and starts complaining. They complain about who didn't do their sidework, why something wasn't prepped, or the traffic. And even if the music was pumping and everything was humming along up to that point, that negative energy starts to take over the whole team. Things tend to quiet down around negative people, mostly because no one wants to engage them. And a quiet kitchen is not a successful kitchen.

These people are energy vampires, and there's only one way to defeat them - you have to pump more positive energy into the kitchen than the negative energy they bring with them. Great leaders create far more energy than they consume. Even when you're coaching someone on a way to improve, you can avoid draining energy from them if you stay away from focusing on policies and pointing out all their mistakes.

"A leader is never energy-neutral. You are either a fountain or a drain."

Jim Sullivan

Mistakes need to be corrected, no doubt, and they will be - you just need to do more celebrating than criticizing.

How can you add more positive energy into the kitchen today? Are you an "energy vampire?" Think about what side of the energy spectrum you're on and how you might be able to be the high tide that lifts all boats when you get to work.

Integrity

Simply put, this means doing what you say you're going to do. Kitchens thrive when there are systems that drive repetition, and therefore consistency. There is no such thing as a leader who asks their team to do one thing and then does something else – that's just a bad boss.

"Every morning you have a choice. Are you going to be a positive thinker or a negative thinker? Positive thinking will energize you."

Jon Gordon,
The Energy Bus

Your integrity depends on:

- being professional

- treating people fairly and consistently

- being approachable

- solving problems, especially when people ask for help

Confidence

Even in the best restaurants, things can get crazy. A rush that comes out of nowhere, a short staff, 86'd product…it can pile up and threaten the sanity of the whole team. And in those dark moments, people need to believe in something or someone. They need to believe it will get better. They need hope.

So how do you become that someone that people turn to at the worst times? Confidence.

When you stay calm and focused on the task at hand, shunning the drama and fear that comes with a shift gone wrong, you will be that light of hope for everyone to grab onto. The future is a great place where everything is OK, and the confident leader knows that and resides there.

"Happiness never decreases by being shared."

Buddha

Get On Deck

If you're working on doing everything you need to do to be a great leader and are ready to be considered for a promotion, you have to let someone know. You have to put your name in the hat. You can't be picked for the job if you're not standing in line.

"Opportunities are like busses... there's always another one coming."

Richard Branson

Renegade Cooks don't wait for things to get better or for someone to notice them. They take credit and make requests.

This is the last piece of Being the Next in Line: showing ambition. Remember, you want to be the obvious choice when the time comes. You want to build the characteristics of good leaders, you want to do your current job well, and you want to have your hand up.

Plan your approach carefully, however. Walking up to the General Manager during a dinner rush and saying, "I think I deserve to be a manager," isn't going to cut it. It's not about feeling entitled, it's about being ambitious. Showing maturity in the way you ask could very well clinch the job for you.

How can you get through loud and clear? Any of the following will help you raise your hand without coming across the wrong way. Let them know that:

- you love working there

- you want to work there for a long time

- you're not planning on moving out of the area

- your schedule is wide open and won't be changing anytime soon

- you've been working on helping everyone on the team be successful

- you genuinely want to know what you can do better

- you understand that a position might not be open right now, but that you want to be in the mix when the next opportunity comes

Remember, that next promotion is yours – just stop worrying about what you do and focus instead on who you are.

Summary

- Being predictable – by being on time and accepting all requests – is the first step to building trust.

- Behavioral skills get you promoted much faster than technical skills.

- You don't need permission – or a title – to be a leader.

- Leaders know they're depended upon, so they make decisions that benefit the Guests and the team. They also stay focused on preventing problems and inspiring others to follow them.

- Craft a message that communicates you're interested in moving up – make sure you don't sound entitled – and share it at an appropriate time.

Few of the ideas expressed in the preceding chapters are groundbreaking or revolutionary. In fact, most are not. The vast majority are best practices for developing as a person and as an employee in the restaurant industry that I've learned over many years in the business.

As a cook or chef, you may even be familiar with some of these techniques for moving ahead in your career. It's my hope that you also came across some new ideas that you can combine with your own.

Most importantly, combine them to become a Renegade. Rebel against the common process of being employed in a kitchen and against the many examples of how to work that typical cooks set for you. You make products every day; now it's time to make yourself the product. One of my favorite sayings is that there's a Chicken Caesar Salad on every menu, so it's up to the people in the restaurant to differentiate one place to eat from another. Don't be a Caesar Salad - there is only one you. Shake up the perceptions others have of you and look for ways to surprise them with your new spirit of success.

FINAL THOUGHTS

Spend some time thinking about the
Characteristics of a *Renegade Cook*:

- Passion

- Standards

- Presentation

- Communication

- Timing

- Handle a Rush

- Consistency

- Attention to Detail

- Attack Tickets

- Awareness

- Be Proactive

- Lead Others

- Accountability

What do you do well? What can you improve?
Who can help you work on the things you might
not be a natural at?

Remember that you need to meet expectations before you can exceed them. That's the idea behind the first of the Rules of Raises, and for each rule, there's a step you can take to earn that next raise.

The Rules	The Plan
You already get paid for what you're supposed to do.	Know what your boss wants you to do. Do what your boss wants you to do
You have to do more to earn more.	Stand out by exceeding expectations.
Your boss is always worried about spending more labor dollars	Save the restaurant money.
Building a case for a raise is up to you.	Ask for a raise.

This plan is progressive. It works best when you take it one step at a time and don't rush it. Don't move on to the next step until you know you're "good to go" with the current one. How will you know? Self-assessment is great, but you can also ask for feedback from peers and supervisors.

Partner with supervisors to help you develop the leadership skills you'll need to move up. Remember, you don't need a title to be a leader. But you do need to show that you can lead others before you can be trusted with a promotion.

Leaders:

- lead others to a common goal
- treat everyone fairly
- select the best person to hire out of a pool of applicants
- make culture thrive
- include others in decisions
- prevent problems from ever happening
- solve the problems that do occur
- have a sense of awareness that exceeds everyone else's
- prioritize based on the needs of Guests, then others, then self

Your future is definitely one of those situations in which you get out of it what you put into it. You'll need to work on becoming a *Renegade Cook* every shift. The best way to do that is to refresh yourself on your plan before each shift so you're in the right frame of mind.

Hopefully you've found some great new ideas in this book, but ask yourself: will you remember them in 30 days? The energy that you built while reading the book can disappear within a month if you don't keep going back to it. Write down which ideas impacted you the most, then read through them at work. Set reminders for specific parts of the action plan in your phone. Rip a page out and tape it to your bathroom mirror. Make the cover of the book your profile picture. Paint *"Renegade Cook"* on the side of your car. Whatever works for you! Just don't let the ideas and the energy fade away.

Find the techniques that appeal most to you and will work best for you. Use them and hone them and make them your own. Stay positive when there's a temporary obstacle in your way. Soon, your successes will start to pile up.

You won't be a typical cook anymore; you'll stand out because of the way you behave and perform at work, and people will recognize you for what you are: a *Renegade Cook*.

FINAL THOUGHTS

Thank you very much for your purchase of this book and support of the Renegade philosophy. I'd love to hear how it works for you.

Please send us your stories of becoming a *Renegade Cook!*

Email: **info@bearenegadecook.com**
Twitter: **@BeARenegadeCook**

Bonus Section
Quick Tips for Cooks

Take action with these tips. Not every single one will be right for you, but we hope you can find a few tips to give your journey to becoming a *Renegade Cook* a boost.

Come back here often!

8 Ways to Be Predictable – In a Good Way

1. Show up 5 minutes early every shift.

2. Keep schedule requests to a minimum.

3. Same for switching shifts that have already been scheduled.

4. Arrive in the correct uniform. Don't finish getting ready at work – show up ready to go.

5. Leave the drama at home. Don't be a roller coaster – happy one day, pissed off the next.

6. Keep talking - nobody knows what quiet cooks are thinking about, which means they're unpredictable. Keep up the call and response, and get into conversations when you can - even if it's just small talk.

7. Follow the recipe.

8. Don't skate on your sidework.

Don't Complain About Guests!

Pay attention to what vibe you're putting out there. It's one thing to say, "That rush killed me! My feet died. They're dead." It's a whole other thing to say things like:

- "Oh great - another idiot who thinks they're gluten-free!"

- "This ticket has 2 app samplers on it - I hate those! How much food do these people need?"

- "If we wanted you to order this sandwich with no tomato or cheese, sub ham, with sourdough, we would have put it on the menu that way!"

- A filet well-done? I might as well drop it on the floor and step on it."

You're here to make Guests happy - even when you don't agree with their choices.

Pre-Shift Checklist

1. Know what to expect. Find out what the sales forecast is and if there are any special events.

2. Identify your team. Who else are you working with? What are their strengths and weaknesses? When do they come in? When do they leave? Are the right people in the right stations?

3. Prepare your station. Check all your equipment. Stock all food, utensils, plates, etc.

4. Go over any notes you've taken on things you want to make sure you do or improve during your shifts.

Passion for Food

Being passionate about food creates happy Guests, and the people you work with will take notice.

1. Lost the spark for food? Try to rekindle your love for cooking for others. What did you enjoy most in the past, and how can you bring that back in your current position?

2. Learn more about food any way you can: read books, watch videos online, check out the millions of cooking shows on TV, cook for friends and family – whatever!

3. Taste your food! All the time. Is it seasoned correctly? Are the flavors coming together right? Is it fresh? It doesn't matter if it's French fries or a scratch sauce, you shouldn't serve it if you haven't tasted it.

4. Learn from someone who's not at work. If you're not learning anything new, find someone who can change that. Take a cooking class – my local food bank offers classes that are appropriate for anyone. Community colleges, culinary schools, and private chefs all have classes as well. Or do a stage at a restaurant that intrigues you. Learn some new techniques or flavor combinations to keep your curiosity about food thriving.

Get Help

Ask for help when you need it during a busy shift! Renegade Cooks enthusiastically accept help from others – and they even seek it out. When your focus is on the happiness of the Guest, nothing will hold you back from getting help to make sure the quality of the food and the speed of service don't suffer.

7 Ways to Show the FOH Some Love

1. Answer their calls immediately.

2. Make them something fun "off menu" for their shift meal.

3. Has a server gotten through a few shifts without any mistakes or been especially helpful to the kitchen? Hand them a $5 gift card for coffee and tell them they did a great job. It might be the best $5 investment you make.

4. Make the refire first; ask questions later.

5. On a folding tent-style card, write, "Hi, I'm Mickey (or whatever your name is). Let me know if you need anything." Place it in the window at your station.

6. Double check your orders to make sure the food you sell is correct – especially when there are modifiers.

7. Don't let food die in the window. Call for a runner – nicely.

BONUS SECTION FOR COOKS

Clean Like a Renegade

Ready for a simple way to stand out? Make the kitchen shine!

- Offer to make a daily/weekly/monthly cleaning schedule for equipment, walls, and coolers. All 3 timelines are important – you're not going to pull all the food out of the walk-in every day to scrub shelves, but it needs to be done periodically.

- Identify the tools you need to clean things right. Would a nylon brush be helpful? Steel scrubbers? A mean oven cleaner? Make a list and ask your boss to order what you need.

- Find hacks for cleaning things quicker and better. Watch the other cooks, ask your friends who cook, or search on Twitter or Reddit for tricks.

Extra Bonus Section
Tips for Managers, Supervisors, & Trainers

Use these tips to help your team continually learn the value of executing better and taking the initiative for their development. Coach them to identify success as the happiness of your Guests, not just the completion of a task or process.

Build a Renegade Restaurant!

Use *The Renegade Cook* in your next:

- Pre-Shift Huddle
- All-Team Meeting
- Manager Meeting
- One-on-One Coaching Session

Use these techniques to help improve the support you provide your BOH teams! Over time, watch the positive effect it has on food quality and presentation, sales, and turnover!

Supply Line

Good leaders remove obstacles for their teams. An easy one? Making sure the BOH has all the tools they need to be successful.

EXTRA BONUS SECTION FOR LEADERS

I always ask cooks if there are enough thermometers for everyone in their kitchen, and the answer is almost always, "No." Once they stop laughing, that is. And yet keeping food at safe temperatures is usually a top food safety standard in every restaurant.

Do a supply check to find out what you might be able to provide to help cooks do their job better and more efficiently. The best way to find out is to ask them! Another good way is to listen to your kitchen, especially during a rush. Are they asking the dishwasher for ramekins? Do they reuse sauté pans when they shouldn't?

Check for:

- Plenty of thermometers

- Clean towels for every shift

- Cleaning and sanitizing chemicals

- Measuring cups and spoons

- Good knives and steels

- Enough cutting boards

- Aprons, jackets, and other parts to the uniform

- Pans and utensils

- Storage containers

- Pens and sharpies

- Plateware

Get Fired Up About Food

It's so easy to get caught up in the process of making food for other people - the steps in the recipe, the ticket, the repetition - that passion for food can erode. As a leader, you can help cooks keep their passion for alive and remember that they're creating an experience for someone, not just selling a ticket.

Don't know where to start? The best place is in the window. Seeing food at the moment it's handed off to the FOH gives you an opportunity to evaluate it - and if needed - coach your team on their execution. Look at their food. Give them feedback. If it's not right, send it back. When cooks are told to refire food because of presentation or proper cooking, it's a sign that food quality is important.

Make sure cooks have opportunities to taste their food. Servers shouldn't be the only ones who taste menu items; it's important for cooks to know how the final product should taste so they can prepare it correctly - both during prep and during service.

When possible, share feedback from your Guests with the cooks. Encourage your FOH team to do the same. It will help the BOH remember they're cooking for people who enjoy their food. Cooks rarely get to see or hear about the results of their work.

EXTRA BONUS SECTION FOR LEADERS

Refine Your Systems

Because cooks do repetitive work, they despise inefficiency. Remove those obstacles by assessing both your kitchen systems and the kitchen itself.

Systems

Cooks love lists. Lists help them analyze the amount of work left and helps them stay on pace. Those same lists can also be adding work or time to cooks' shifts. Look at prep lists for opportunities like adjusting pars that help them prepare only what they need for the shift. There might also be items that are being prepped in multiple stations, like diced onions. It would be much more efficient for one person to prep all the onions for the kitchen than having three cooks do it at different times. One more thing to look at: Cleaning Lists. Do they make sense? Are they balanced between different shifts and stations? Could cleaning tasks be grouped together when they are in the same area or use the same cleaning materials?

Space

Optimizing the kitchen layout is all about making cooks more efficient. The goal is to reduce the number of steps they make, whether it's by eliminating trips or shortening the distance they need to walk. Look for:

- Back-ups that can be stored closer to the line

- Ingredients that can be stored closer to the prep area

- Getting a cart to reduce the number of trips made

- Storage at each station, so line cooks don't have to cross over each other

- More room for pans, plates, and other items so they don't need to be restocked as frequently

EXTRA BONUS SECTION FOR LEADERS

Be Inclusive

If you can only remember one phrase as a leader, let it be, "Make everyone feel important."

Ask yourself how well you include cooks in your shift management and people development, both as a group and as individuals. Do you:

- Speak to every cook, every shift?

- Include BOH team members in sales contests?

- Provide the same training to the BOH as the FOH?

- Treat BOH team members with different primary languages equally?

- Spend time equally with BOH team members of each position?

- Coach each individual, even if you don't feel connected with them?

- Deliver performance reviews on time?

- Share a clear career path with BOH teams and provide the support they need to move up?

One More Thing

Want to change your relationship with the kitchen in a powerful way? Make this simple change:

> Don't ask *if* you can help,
> ask *how* you can help.

Any FOH manager who stops at the end of the line on a busy night and asks, "Do you need any help?" will always get the same answer: "Nope!" Unfortunately, they're in the weeds, and you know it. So, avoid the "yes or no" question by asking *how* you can help instead. Even if it's just going to get a backup from the walk-in, you're saving a step and showing them you're paying attention and are ready to step in.

About Matt Nelson

In over 20 years in the hospitality business, Matt Nelson has loaded dish racks, cooked on hot lines, led BOH and FOH teams as a manager, and created training programs for several years in corporate training departments. He's the founder and president of Modern Training and Development, Inc., a company committed to helping the hospitality industry build best-in-class training programs. "ModTD" has built its reputation on crafting highly-customized training solutions that bring new ideas to clients while keeping the voice of the brand, making it feel like the programs were developed internally. Matt believes in creating training programs that are streamlined and simple for managers to facilitate while helping their teams build skills and feel prepared to do their jobs.

His company partners with brands to help develop training programs on-demand as well as through ongoing support with the Virtual Training Department service. In addition to those training strategy, print, and online learning solutions, Matt delivers highly customized presentations on leadership, training, and all the topics found in *The Renegade Cook*. You can reach him at moderntd.com.

More Renegade Cook!

Live Seminars and Workshops

Bring the insight of *The Renegade Cook* to your teams! Perfect for annual conferences and other gatherings, Matt delivers a memorable presentation with just the right amount of humor. Attendees come away with dozens of real, immediately usable tools and tactics for leading their culinary teams to greater success.

In addition to an energizing presentation on stage, we make sure the positive results you envision become a reality, with next-day and 30-day follow-up activities you can facilitate so nothing gets forgotten. Take your kitchen leadership to another level and leave your competition for customers and employees in the dust!

Custom Training

Partner with Matt and his team to develop customized training programs and materials based on *The Renegade Cook*. From online courses to leader guides to tools for cooks, create an ecosystem of training and ongoing inspiration for your culinary teams!

Contact us at **info@bearenegadecook.com**

Learn More. *Earn More.*

RENEGADE HOSPITALITY GROUP

Visit *renegadehospitality.com* to learn more about our training, tools and consulting that elevate people, performance and profits, including:

Live Seminars

Consulting

Custom Training Solutions

Renegade products including books, DVDs, and CDs

Free downloads, e-newsletters, blogs, videos and more digital content

The Renegade Server Book Discussion Guide is available free online at *Renegadehospitality.com* and *Sullivision.com.*

Follow us

Learn More. *Earn More.*

Renegade Server In-A-Box

Renegade Server In-A-Box is the complete restaurant training system based on the book you hold in your hands. It is a comprehensive toolkit that will help trainers and managers train the sales and service skills from The Renegade Server to new employees and existing teams alike. It includes a print version of the book as well as:

The Renegade Server 3-CD Audiobook
The Renegade Server LIVE 88 minute DVD and a
CD-ROM which contains:

- Complete slide deck presentation that teaches the Renegade philosophy and tactics in an interactive classroom format

- Leader's Guide including step-by-step instruction for conducting the training

- Learner's Workbooks for trainees to capture and keep the lessons of *The Renegade Server*

- Classroom handouts and flashcards
- Meeting & incentive templates
- Much, much more! Visit

Renegadehospitality.com for details.

RENEGADE HOSPITALITY

Learn More. *Earn More.*

Live Seminars & Workshops

Find out why over 20,000 people attend Tim Kirkland's engaging and informative seminars every year!

Tim's delivery is professional, engaging and balanced with real-world experience and good-natured humor. Attendees are guaranteed to come away with dozens of real, immediately useable tools and tactics, not just 'inspiration' from the stage (though there's plenty of that, too). All of our content is intricately tailored for each client and designed to specifically address the goals, expectations, needs and culture of the organization.

> *"Tim presented a keynote address and two breakout sessions at our National Training Camp. His message was clear, concise, and completely in line with the message of our convention. Tim gave our audience members simple tactics that they could use right away to build their businesses.* **By far, Tim was the best convention speaker I have seen** *at any Buffalo Wild Wings convention."*
>
> **- Nikki Fuchs de Calderon**
> Director of Management Development,
> Buffalo Wild Wings

> *"Tim Kirkland allowed us the opportunity to wrap up our 2 ½ day franchisee convention in a powerful way. Tim understood our unique audience of corporate employees, franchisees and managers and was able to connect with them on a real level. We solicit feed-back from our attendees through an online survey after the event and* **Tim Kirkland's ratings were the highest we've ever seen from a guest speaker.** *I highly recommend Tim to your organization if you're looking for a high-energy, motivated speaker who can really connect with the audience and share a powerful message."*
>
> **- Heather Neary**
> Chief Marketing Officer, Auntie Anne's, Inc.

Tim speaks with authority on a variety of subjects including Customer Service, Salesmanship, Leadership, Marketing, Change Management and Team Development.

Learn More. *Earn More.*

The Renegade Server **LIVE DVD**

In this live version of the best-selling book, author Tim Kirkland brings his unique money-making insights to life with thought-provoking, real-life anecdotes, high-energy interactions and good-natured humor. Filmed live on stage during one of Tim's popular Renegade seminars, this is THE tool that helps servers and bartenders make more money while helping managers and owners train the skills that drive sales and intensify guest loyalty. Show it to your team today, and make more money tomorrow!

Tip Clips Digital DVD

This high-impact digital training tool takes uncommon insights from the best-selling book and brings them directly to the restaurant floor. Comprised of thirty-three, 1- to 4-minute-long digital video clips, this is the mobile training tool that will put the power of *The Renegade Server* in your team's hands every shift. The CD-ROM features Tim Kirkland communicating the most important parts of the book in both .mp4 and Quick Time file formats so you can train on any computer OR mobile device. PLUS - a second bonus Video DVD disc for use on the big screen! This set of powerful clips makes an invaluable addition to any restaurant training program.

The Renegade Server AudioBook

This is the 3-CD audio version of Tim Kirkland's bestselling book for full-service servers, bartenders and restaurant operators, read by the author. Use your travel time or exercise time to get smarter, faster and make more money.

Check out The Renegade Server Coaching Handbook

This supplement to The Renegade Server teaches managers how to implement the crucial lessons and tactics contained in the best-selling book in ways that front-line teams will value and adopt. It also extends the philosophies and strategies from the original book and applies them to the nature and function of leadership itself. Full of ideas, tools, meetings, incentives and discussion guides, this valuable addition will help you elevate not just your team's performance, but yours as a leader, as well.

Where Leaders Go to Learn™

Get Smart. Stay Smart. Learn How.

Since 2001 Sullivision.com has designed and delivered targeted training tools that drive revenue for successful foodservice and retail brands around the globe. Companies that use our products, programs and services include:

Walt Disney Company, Starbucks, Target, Chili's, Wal-Mart, Panera Bread, Applebee's, Marriott, McDonald's, Denny's, IHOP, Wagamama, Pizza Hut, Buffalo Wild Wings, Subway, The Cheesecake Factory, Five Guys Burger and Fries, HMSHost, Darden Restaurants, and many more.

Visit us online at Sullivision.com to see our complete catalog of training tools, learning resources and leadership insight. You can also see a complete list of our customized workshops and keynote presentations for your next leadership conference. Our website resources include:
• Apps • Books • DVDs • Posters • Videos • ELearning • Consulting • Seminars
• Exclusive section for Multiunit Leaders and Multiunit Franchisees

Follow us on:

Order our products safely and securely online anytime at Sullivision.com

154

Where Leaders Go to Learn™

Power Tools for Managers

Every Foodservice Manager Needs these DVDs for their Team and their Restaurants

Jumpstart: How to Plan and Execute Effective Pre-Shift Meetings is an award-winning 60 minute DVD that will show your managers the wrong and right ways to deliver effective and goal-oriented "pep rallies" before each shift for every department. Watch and learn realistic examples of how to jumpstart service, sales and cost-control before every shift. Loaded with bonus training features too. Used in over 50,000 restaurants worldwide. Order online at Sullivision.com or Amazon.

The Shift: How to Plan It, Lead It, Make It Pay

will help every foodservice manager understand the architecture of the revenue-generating shift. They'll learn how to break down period goals to shift targets, the best practices related to leadership before, during and after the shift, how to coach each member through each shift, and how to make every customer interaction positive in the dining room, drive-through or counter. This 60-minute DVD is used in over 45,000 restaurants worldwide. Order online at Sullivision. com or Amazon.

Buy Both & Save!
Jumpstart DVD
AND The Shift DVD

This Dynamic Duo of training DVDs are guaranteed to drive more revenue in any restaurant, every shift. Effective for both full-service and quick-service food service operations. Get them both for a great price at **Sullivision.com**

The Two All-Time Best-Selling Books in Foodservice: Over 400,000 Copies Sold!

Multiunit Leadership: The 7 Stages of Operating Successful Multiunit Businesses

Based on research with over 500 High Performing Multiunit Managers, Area Directors and Multiunit Franchisees, this best-selling book will teach you how to:

- *Master the seven competencies of effective multiunit leaders*
- *Motivate diverse managers and teams to serve better and sell more*
- *Deliver high-impact unit visits instead of merely "inspecting" them*
- *Build more revenue across multiple units and markets*
- *Execute annual goals with habitual consistency every shift*
- *Select and develop the best unit managers*
- *Effectively manage time and activities in a 24/7 world*
- *Unify brand standards across multiple units, and More!*

304 pages, illustrated and available at Sullivision.com and Amazon. Go to Sullivision.com for additional Multiunit Leadership resources including DVDs, audiobooks and the Multiunit-Leadership-in-a-Box customizable training kit.

Fundamentals: 9 Ways to Be Brilliant at the New Basics

Teach your unit managers the most effective ways to execute the fundamentals of service, selling, marketing, training and cost-control in this perennial best seller. Learn the most creative new ways to Increase Sales, Energize Service, Build Strong Teams, Market Smarter, Watch Your Waste, Lead Smarter and Execute Every Shift. This 200 page, illustrated, hardcover book is the perfect training tool for every executive, GM, and store manager. It's the gift that can be opened again and again! Includes free online Discussion Guides, templates, and supporting videos for every chapter. Only $22.00. Used in over 100,000 businesses worldwide.

See our entire training product catalog and more at **Sullivision.com**

NOTES

NOTES

NOTES

NOTES

NOTES

NOTES

NOTES

NOTES

NOTES

NOTES

NOTES

NOTES